Speeches
and Presentations

JANE WILLIS

WARD LOCK

A WARD LOCK BOOK

First published in the UK 1996
by Ward Lock
Wellington House 125 Strand LONDON WC2R 0BB

A Cassell Imprint

Copyright © Jane Willis 1996

Distributed in the United States
by Sterling Publishing Co., Inc.
387 Park Avenue South, New York, NY 10016-8810

Distributed in Australia
by Capricorn Link (Australia) Pty Ltd
2/13 Carrington Road, Castle Hill NSW 2154

A British Library Cataloguing in Publication Data block for this book
may be obtained from the British Library

ISBN 0 7063 7496 7

Typeset by Business Color Print, Welshpool, Powys, Wales
Printed and bound in Great Britain by Biddles, Guildford

Contents

CHAPTER ONE   AN OVERVIEW   5

CHAPTER TWO   REPARING YOURSELF   13

CHAPTER THREE   PREPARING YOUR MATERIAL   36

CHAPTER FOUR   PREPARING AND PRACTISING YOUR DELIVERY   56

CHAPTER FIVE   GIVING YOUR PRESENTATION   70

CHAPTER SIX   FEEDBACK AND AFTERTHOUGHTS   91

INDEX   96

ACKNOWLEDGEMENTS

My thanks to James Willis for material on 'computer viruses', to Jonathan Willis for his example in 'Introducing a speaker' and to Naeema Adal for typing the manuscript.

CHAPTER ONE

An overview

THE SPEAKER AND THE SPEECH

Welcome to this self-help manual. I hope you enjoy and have fun practising the exercises, and that you find the contents of help with your business and social presentation skills.

There are two principal factors involved in the making of a public speaker: there is the person who makes the speech, and there is the message that the speaker delivers.

Have you ever considered how unnatural it is to stand up in front of a crowd of people and speak? Imagine it now. Sit in a chair and close your eyes. Pretend that you have been asked to appear in front of a large gathering. How do you feel? Does it remind you of anything? Perhaps you are back at school, being brought to task over some misdemeanour. Or maybe you forgot your lines in the school or college play. Do you recall stumbling over the words of a passage of text that you had been asked to read aloud? Maybe, on the other hand, you were a model pupil, a good actor, or a fluent sight-reader, enjoying audience attention. Whatever the memories, positive or negative, you will probably remember and feel something.

This book suggests ideas which will improve your technical expertise in the field of public speaking. However, the most valuable asset that we all possess is ourselves and that personality, in my view, must never be lost; after all, it is the person who sells the product.

Some people being more extrovert than others may thrive on audience attention, while others shy away from it. Unfortunately, we are not always offered the luxury of being able to choose whether or not we are to be placed in front of the footlights. We may, by the nature of our work, be expected to give presentations, deliver a speech (for example, at the Parent-teacher Association), give an introduction or make an appeal. If we encourage self-awareness, we are enabled to change or modify that about ourselves which can be changed and learn to come to terms with that which can't. Self-acceptance can be a big step forward towards the confidence front.

Technical perfection in speaking is insufficient on its own: it needs to be tempered with self-knowledge. Partly because it is personal warmth and contact with our listeners that strengthen communication; and also because self-awareness enables us to feel happier within ourselves while delivering a talk and to become sincere speakers.

COMMUNICATION

As a teacher of public-speaking skills, clients sometimes say to me, 'It's stupid of me to get so nervous at the thought of giving this presentation.' They use similar adjectives: 'foolish', 'silly', 'ridiculous', thus mentally berating themselves for their 'unacceptable' feelings. However, they are expressing very natural feelings about something that is very unnatural to do. Speaking in public is a brave act!

When communicating in pairs or small groups, we interact through speech and body language. If, however, we stand apart from a group or speak in front of a crowd, all this changes. Audiences tend to react collectively, taking their leads from each other. The speaker, on the other hand, stands apart and is to some degree alone. It is from this unhelpful and unnatural vantage point that audience contact has to be made: a contact that will encourage an ambience conducive to both the needs of the speaker and the audience. Little wonder then that nerves are affected.

In this manual I do not offer a panacea against nervousness. Rather, suggestions are made of ways of helping you to ease these feelings, while at the same time accepting their presence and trusting the challenge they can offer. The more speeches you make, the more polished your performance is likely to become, and the more confident you are likely to feel. So take every opportunity offered to speak in public, whether it be reading the lesson in church, addressing the Girl Guides, giving an after-dinner speech or a business presentation. Do it – because while there is no guarantee that this will be the cure-all for nerves, it will surely help simply by virtue of repetition.

IMPROVING YOUR SKILLS

The technical side of public speaking is not easy. Surprisingly, there are those who assume that oratory is an innate gift bestowed on the privileged few. It is a subject that can be studied like any other subject, and is often undertaken most diligently by those who appear to have a leaning towards eloquence.

In my experience as a teacher, there are some clients who are conscientious, consistent hard workers. They are the ones who gain ground in this subject, gradually becoming more self-assured, and thoroughly enjoying the whole work experience. There are those however, who, perhaps owing to work commitments, claim to be too busy to complete the preparations. They are sometimes the ones who subsequently become stressed when their presentations at work or elsewhere are imminent, because they are unprepared. I am not underestimating the pressures on the average business person, but it is important to take responsibility for your own learning. There is no magic wand. A teacher cannot answer the question, 'Will I be all right?' The reassurance must come from within you with the knowledge that you have done the very best you can with your abilities.

Practise the exercises in this book methodically, and as regularly as you think is necessary and helpful for you. Find additional material of your own to practise as well. Expand your learning by studying and finding out more. That way you will feel more in control. Learn to enjoy your subject.

A friend of mine, Sally, was about to sit her teacher's finals. One of the papers was Sociology, a subject that she had always found extremely difficult. Convinced in her own mind that she was going to fail, she visualized fellow students scribbling away at their answers, while she sat there without a clue.

A few days before the exam, Sally was sifting through her wardrobe when her fingers touched a green silk, very expensive designer frock, that she had only worn twice. Both times had been happy occasions: her brother's wedding and a dinner party. Sally recalled the many compliments she had received as a result of wearing this frock. She discovered to her surprise that she was smiling for the first time in quite a while. It was then Sally had her idea. She would wear the frock to sit the Sociology paper.

When the morning arrived, Sally got up extra early, allowing herself plenty of time to do her make-up and arrange her hair with care. She then put on her beautiful and elegant green frock. She wore her smartest patent high heels, not forgetting earrings and scent to complete the stunning ensemble. Then she made her way to the university, feeling smart but slightly incongruous among the jean-clad students gathered outside the examination room. They greeted her with some surprise when they saw her unusual outfit, but undaunted she took her place among the others. As she waited for the invigilator to utter the dreaded words, 'You may turn over your paper and begin,' she recalled those two splendid occasions when she had felt so good about herself. She asked herself how she felt now: 'I feel all right. I've done the best I can with my revision. The rest is in the lap of the gods.' Sally passed the exam.

I am a great believer in affirmations, or auto-suggestions as they used to be called. They can be a confidence aid. In Sally's case, she worked from the outside (her physical appearance) to help give her an inside confidence. This may have helped her pass the examination. Even if she had failed, Sally had made her path easier and calmer by thinking positively.

In this manual you will come across the following short sentences:

1 I am relaxed and confident.
2 My neck is free of tension.
3 I am filling my body with energy.
4 I am releasing my sound into the room.
5 I shall be heard.

Although in the book these are used as an exercise for breath and voice, you can practise them to help boost morale. Better still, you may like to invent your own affirmations. They must not be parroted, but arise from an inner belief in what you are saying. By focusing on your words, you can develop a genuine and positive outlook. This may hold you in good stead and empower your performance.

When I was teaching in schools, it was usually the smart-dressed members of staff who attracted the most interest from teachers and pupils alike. Good grooming is essential for presentation and is of course part of any presentation and, as my story illustrates, it can do wonders for the ego!

The original duty of The Groom of the Stole, according to the third edition of *Brewer's Dictionary of Phrase and Fable*, was not only 'To invest the king in his state-robe', but 'he had also to hand him his shirt when he dressed.'

While it is important and beneficial for the speaker to be outwardly well clad, the basic garment should not be overlooked. I refer to the grooming of clear, well-enunciated speech. Only when this is present, is the outward ensemble complete.

There are some speakers and performers who appear to be under the misconception that volume is all and, while this wash of loud sound undoubtedly reaches their audience, unfortunately in some cases, intelligibility does not. Clarity of speech helps to carry the voice forward and so aids projection. By working the jaw, mouth and tongue muscles, you are mobilizing the face and giving it extra life and vigour. Chapter 2, Preparing yourself, contains exercises that will help you achieve breath control, clarity and power.

Unless there is a clinical reason for it, sloppy, inarticulate speech is inexcusable. It does nothing for the speaker and even less for the poor suffering audience who have to sit and endure blanketed sound, straining to make sense of it.

Words are composed of vowels and consonants and it is very often the consonants, particularly those at the ends of words, that are neglected. They are sometimes indistinct, or left out almost entirely. I am not suggesting that words should be delivered with over-punctiliousness as this will sound pedantic, stilted, and unnatural.

Although, of course, it is desirable that language should flow, being mindful of pronunciation and diction is important.

Use the exercises you will find in this manual. By thorough, regular practice (little and often), the muscles in the mouth will be re-educated, thus enabling you to have clearer enunciation. Once familiarity with the exercises is achieved, focusing on speech content should in itself act as a more automatic reminder, as well as being a motivating factor towards clearer speech. Opening the mouth to let out the vowel sounds, and remembering to finish the end sounds of words, will encourage an improved style of delivery and a positive audience response. Mumbling can also reflect lack of confidence. Once this is transmitted to an audience, the speaker loses credibility.

Another word for message is communication. The skills that you develop will be the tool kit used by you the speaker to impart the message to your audience. Structurally, the speech you are to give needs to be clear, well defined and easy to understand. Added ingredients may include: humour, anecdotes, and the use of visual aids. Suggestions are given in Chapter 3 for ways of preparing a presentation for both business and social events.

The effectiveness of a speech (business or social) is largely dependent on the manner in which it is delivered. A pleasing tonality of voice, use of emphasis, pause, pace and volume can enhance a presentation and greatly increase audience interest. This may be of vital importance for those involved in business as well as social occasions.

Learning the art of colourful delivery can increase personal magnetism, and can also prove to be an invaluable business and social asset on or off the platform.

SUMMARY

1 The public speaker needs to address mental attitude and to work on the skills of making contact with the listeners. These can be enhanced by developing and maintaining a positive approach, self-awareness and sincerity.

2 Learning self-acceptance and being prepared to work towards realistic goals encourage a sense of perspective, while using practice for performance improvement can help to overcome extreme feelings of nervousness.

3 Attention should be paid to smart physical grooming. In addition, the speech needs to be clear and articulate, thus sharpening the speaker's image and ensuring good communication with the audience.

4 A speech needs to be structured, stimulating and audience-friendly – complemented by a well-modulated delivery.

It was Bacon (in *Essays: of Ceremonies and Respects*) who said, 'A wise man will make more opportunities than he finds.' If you want to get ahead and be noticed, public speaking will help you do just that. However, you need to put yourself forward and maximize your assets. I hope that this manual will act as a spring-board. Good luck!

CHAPTER TWO

Preparing yourself

COPING WITH NERVES

John to himself:

'I feel awful! Look at all those people out there waiting for me to get up and confound them with wisdom!

'I just know I'll be a failure. Remember Sheffield? How can I forget! Losing two sheets of notes up there on the platform and drying up completely like an idiot. I just wanted to die. I want to die now! My heart's pounding so hard, I'm sure the audience can hear. And my hands are so wet and shaky. I keep wanting to swallow. I bet I'll do the same as last time and drop my notes.

'Now what do I say at the beginning? Introductions are supposed to be riveting. I wish I'd rehearsed the wretched thing more.

'Just look at that smooth, cool guy who's going to speak after me. I'd like to wipe that self-satisfied smirk off his face. Or is it that he just looks confident? Why, why, why didn't I spend more time on this, instead of being persuaded to paint the kitchen?

'Oh no, the chairman's finished speaking. They're all clapping. Is the clapping for me? It is? I think I'm going to be sick!'

Most of us experience nerves in a stressful situation. It is normal. We become charged with adrenaline which can spur us on. When speaking in public, this adrenaline helps to create a good, energetic performance. But feeling incapacitated by nerves is serious.

First look back . . .

If this has ever happened to you, ask yourself why. Did you feel under-rehearsed? Or was it the sight of impassive faces that terrified you? Maybe the feelings arose because the recollection of your last talk was one of endless mistakes.

It is important to remember that with growth there is also change. What happened to us last year may not repeat itself this time. We can learn lessons from our mistakes and experiences and so grow as individuals. Learning to adopt a more positive perception of ourselves will help us to function with more assertiveness and with more confidence.

. . . then look forward

Here are some suggestions to consider before you prepare your next speech. Assess a speech you have made that went wrong. Share it with a friend. Talk it through. Discuss how you felt. Jot these points down on paper and think of ways in which you might improve. Now, sweep that bad memory away.

BE GENTLE WITH YOURSELF

Pat yourself on the back for points that have gone well. Avoid aiming at perfection, it may increase a state of anxiety. Remember it is only through practice that you will improve. The more speeches you make, the better you can become.

BE PREPARED!

Rehearsal is vital. The better prepared you are in advance the less agitated and unsure you are likely to feel when the day arrives.

BE A LISTENER

Listen and watch good speakers as much as possible. Notice the way they construct and deliver their sentences. The more direct and simple the message, the more readily is it communicated.

Listen for eloquence and economy of speech. Shorter sentences hold impact and are easier to grasp than long ones. They also help to discipline the speaker from straying off the point.

LOOK FORWARD TO YOUR SPEECH

Beforehand, and on the day of the event tell yourself that you are looking forward to making your speech. Keep saying this to yourself until you come to believe it. When you finally stand in front of the audience, say to yourself, 'I am glad to be here. I wish this to go well for you and for me.' This reinforces feelings of goodwill and will express itself through your body language and voice.

EXERCISES TO HELP YOU RELAX

Exercise 1   The shoulders
Standing in a relaxed position, lift the shoulders slightly and tense them. Now relax them by letting them fall. Note the difference. Sometimes we lift the shoulders and tense them without realizing that we are doing so. When the shoulders are tensed, the neck becomes tight and we can feel very uncomfortable and tire more easily.

Exercise 2   The neck
Imagine that you have a very long neck. It is perfectly poised between the shoulders which are relaxed and down. Your chin tucks in naturally and with ease. Now move your head gently and with a feeling of elegance turn

your head to the left. Next gently take the head from the left side to the front. Pause. Now gently take the head to the right side and then to the front. Pause.

Imagine being in front of an audience. Repeat the exercise, pretending you are sweeping your listeners with your eyes. Take it slowly and rhythmically, keeping in your mind a feeling of calmness and dignity.

Exercise 3   The head

Imagine that your head is made of granite. In a standing position, let the head slowly, very slowly fall onto your chest. It feels so heavy that it must succumb to the force of gravity. Keep this feeling with you.

Now for the transformation! Your head is now as light as cotton wool as it floats to an upright position.

Practise this several times to experience the contrast between the feelings of lightness and heaviness.

Exercise 4   A gentle sigh

Standing in a relaxed upright position, inhale slowly and then emit a slow gentle sigh of relief. Think of the sigh as though it were coming from the centre of your body. The shoulders should be down and relaxed. The feeling is one of letting go. As you inhale, place your hands on the lower ribs on either side of your waist and experience the gentle upward and lateral movement of the lower ribs.

Exercise 5   Concentration

Choose an interesting or decorative object that appeals to you – an ornament or flower perhaps. Sit in an easy chair with a well-supporting back, and place the object on a table in front of you. Now fix your mind on it. Take in as much detail as you can: colour, texture, shape and so on. Concentrate, giving it your full attention. Now, resting your head against the back of the chair, close your eyes and place the image of that object in your mind. See if you can recall an accurate likeness. When you are ready, open the eyes.

Exercise 6   *Visualizing an entrance*
Use your dining room table and chairs for this one.

Imagine that you are a guest speaker at a meeting. Around the table are seated business associates. They are waiting for you to take your place among them. Carry a folder and enter the room in a pessimistic manner. Eyes cast down perhaps, the walk uncertain, with rounded or tense shoulders. Walk to the table, place the folder on it and sit. All your movements suggest lack of confidence and assertiveness.

Repeat the exercise. Again you are very tense and unhappy about the prospect of this meeting. But in this instance it is important that you should on no account lose face. You must be seen to be in charge of the situation. To fail would be unthinkable. They must not see how you feel. You are on the defensive. The body is held stiffly. The shoulders are hunched. The face is set and unsmiling. The walk is stilted. You may cough nervously and play with your tie or necklace as you take a seat at the table. You reach over for a drink of water. Your hands are shaking. Visualize the effect all this might have on the others.

You are now entering the room for the third time. On this occasion you are optimistic and positive. The shoulders are relaxed and down and the head is well balanced between the shoulder blades. The eyes sweep the table where the others are seated and they reflect warmth, interest and enthusiasm. Walking to your seat with purpose and drive you place the folder on the table. When seated, you rest your arms on the table with hands lightly clasped. You smile pleasantly. It is a smile that has arisen from a knowledge that your feeling of self-esteem is high.

It tells the others that you are pleased to be among them and are ready to do business.

Exercise 7   Recalling a speech
Sit in a chair and think about a speech that you may have heard in the past. In your mind, recall the audience. How did they react to the talk? Did they appear happy and satisfied or bored and restless? Was the speaker attractive in appearance and manner? If so, why? How did he or she move? Was the voice interesting? Was a message communicated that was clear and concise? Were there amusing breaks, offering light relief?

Now imagine that it is you giving the speech in place of the speaker. It may be a similar talk, given to the same audience. How would you like to be seen? Try to see yourself through the eyes of that audience. Listen to their needs. Think it through stage by stage from the entrance, when you walk to the platform, or rise from your seat, to the applause at the end.

BREATH AND THE VOICE

Breathing for any form of speech is a natural function that we don't normally think about. However, paying it some attention is necessary for those who find it difficult to project their voices easily when speaking in public.

To be heard while addressing an audience, we need to create space in the throat and chest so that the required amount of air can be freely inhaled. When using the voice, the exhaled air is directed through the vibrating vocal cords. The throat, mouth and nose help us to amplify our sound, which would be less audible if it did not pass through these resonators. The mouth and throat should therefore be free of tension, and the nose kept clear and unblocked, in order for the resonators to function effectively.

EXERCISES FOR BREATH CONTROL

Exercise 8 Breathing in

Stand straight but not stiffly. This is important, as good alignment will help promote strong voice production. Remember when you inhale not to raise your shoulders. Doing so will encourage tension in the neck, throat and breathing muscles.

Now feel your ribcage. Ribs form the thorax and are attached at the back to the twelve thoracic vertebrae. Rest one hand on your midriff and the other on your lower ribs that reach round the waist. Breathe in slowly and notice how the hand resting on the midriff moves out slightly. This has happened because the diaphragm, which is a muscular partition that separates the thorax from the abdomen, has contracted and flattened, thereby pushing the belly outwards. Because the lower ribs are more flexible than those higher up, they will flex upwards and outwards by the use of the intercostal muscles that are attached to them.

This muscular activity expands the chest cavity, creating more space for the lungs to fill with air, which is drawn into them through the windpipe, nose and/or mouth.

Exercise 9 Breathing out

Now breathe out slowly and feel the lower ribs gradually relax as the lungs contract. The diaphragm rises and the midriff or belly moves inwards. As this is happening, the transverse abdominal muscles are gently drawn inwards. This contraction of the abdominal muscles is used to help our outgoing breath when we speak, gently supporting the diaphragm and lower ribs, so that sound can be sustained and energized.

Remember: breath in, hand on midriff moves outwards; breath out, hand moves inwards.

Because it is on the outgoing breath that we speak, we aim to balance breath with sound. The moment we start to exhale, we need to use the voice. Aim to achieve this smoothness in the following exercise (Exercise 10). Practising regularly and for short periods should help give you the breath control that is needed when speaking in front of an audience.

Physical tensions and feelings of nervousness may be increased, or even caused by the insufficient intake of air; at times this can result in a sore throat, breathy or strained voice and tailing off at the ends of sentences. Some speakers do not allow themselves breathing space! They take in small gasps of air and do not take advantage of their breathing muscles. The shoulders may rise on inhalation, which encourages the ribs to move in one way only – vertically – and this can constrict the breath. The ribs need to flex vertically and laterally. Raising the arms slightly to the side while practising breathing in may provide a picture of opening out, so that lateral expansion is encouraged.

Exercise 10   *Humming*

HUM. This is a very resonant sound. As you do this become aware of the vibrations by touching your throat, lips and nose.

Now, taking a full breath, increase the volume of the hum. Finally, begin softly and gradually increase the volume until quite loud. Stay relaxed, avoid strain and rest in between exercises.

Exercise 11   *Hoorah!*

Take the word HOORAH! Repeat it several times with freedom and spontaneity. This is a valuable exercise as an aid for overcoming inhibitions. Use your arm to guide your sound forward and have fun with it!

Exercise 12   Sound from your centre
Imagine the sound rising naturally from your midriff or centre as you speak the following sentences. Allow your thoughts to guide the sense of what you are saying. Remember to pause and breathe after each sentence.

1   I am relaxed and confident.

2   My neck is free of tension.

3   I am filling my body with energy.

4   I am releasing my sound into the room.

5   I shall be heard.

THE POWER BEHIND YOUR VOICE

The string of pearls
When speaking in public, the voice needs to be strong without strain or shouting. Your breath is the power behind your voice. Imagine a string of pearls. The string has to be long enough to support the pearls but if that string is weak and breaks, the pearls will scatter all over the floor. So it is with the voice. The string is the breath and the pearls are the words. There must therefore be enough breath-power behind the voice to support the words, otherwise the air will run out and the voice falter and fade. It is important to inhale as much air as necessary. The aim is to flow and we breathe where there are natural pauses in the text.

In order to make sense of content, learn where to punctuate your speech and phrase your words. Do not break your phrases or your speech will become jerky and the sense may be lost.

When your speech is prepared, rehearse it aloud, and initially gauge where you are going to take:
(a) your full-stop pauses (remember you will pause longer and take a fuller breath at your full-stop break) and
(b) your comma pauses and supplementary breaths.

Speak the following exercise. Use this sign / for a comma breath pause and // for a full-stop breath pause.

As you take your breaths during this exercise, imagine that they are gently dropping into the centre of your body, at the waist. Breathe out with the words, aiming to keep the voice sustained all the while. To help you, rest a hand on your midriff as you do this.

Ensure that you are standing straight but be at ease, especially around the top part of your body, the neck, throat and shoulders, which should be relaxed and down. Stand with legs slightly apart, the weight evenly distributed on both feet. Your head needs to be well balanced between the shoulder blades. The chin should not jut out or be pushed too far into the neck. If you were speaking to a fairly large audience you would need to speak a little slower and very clearly.

Exercise 13 Phrasing and pausing 1: Jersey
The state of Jersey is a part of the Channel Islands / and is twelve miles from the coast of France. //

Physical features resemble a mixture of Normandy in France, / and the county of Wiltshire in England. //

The island is small: / nine miles by five, / and divided into twelve parishes.//

Villages are picturesque, / comprising stone-built farms and well-kept houses.// Winding roads are flanked on either side by soft rolling countryside, / small sheltered bays and natural harbours.//

The chief industry is market gardening; / and it is on this island that the well-known Jersey cow is reared. //

French influence on Jersey is reflected in the names of roads, / and of some farms and houses. //

Although Jersey is a self-run state, / having its own legislative assemblies and legal systems, / it still remains part of the British Isles. //

In 1941 Jersey was invaded and occupied by the German forces, / who remained there until 1945 and the ending of the war. //

Exercise 14   Phrasing and pausing 2: The secretary bird
The secretary bird is an African bird of prey. //

It gets its name from the crest of long feathers on top of its head which resemble the old quill pens. //

The plumage is grey and white, / with black hindquarters and black and white bars on the tail. //

It stands four feet tall, / has very long legs and a two-foot long tail. //

Secretary birds feed mainly on insects, / lizards and small snakes. //

The nest is built of sticks and clay, / and is used over a period of a few years. //

The large eggs are laid in August. //

When they are hatched, / the young birds do not leave the nest for about five months. //

Although secretary birds are powerful fliers, / they spend a great deal of their time on the ground. //

Before practising the next exercise, mark where you are going to place your breath pauses. Some of the sentences are quite long and require good breath support.

Exercise 15   Phrasing and pausing 3: The jay
The history and grandeur of England have rested on one bird, the jay. If it were not for this beautiful creature,

Henry VIII's great navy could not have set sail to conquer and help build the great British Empire. For it is the jay that is responsible for the propagation of the English oak, being the only species that commonly plants acorns. This is because, unlike the squirrel, it does not bite off the fruit's tip, thus preventing its germination.

There are more exercises to help you in developing ability to phrase and pause in Chapter 4.

USING THE MUSCLES OF THE FACE

Exercises 16 and 17 will help to develop strong and flexible facial muscles.

Use a mirror to ensure that you are working the lip muscles. With the sound **W** as in **will**, the lips need to be brought well forward into a small circle. For the **ee** sound as in the word **we**, the lips need to be gently drawn back as though you are giving someone a soft smile. Avoid overstretching the mouth as this will create tension, the very thing you need to avoid. Thorough but gentle exercise is what is needed. The same principles apply to the piece of verse. These exercises should be practised regularly prior to a public-speaking engagement.

Exercise 16   Mouth and lip muscles

1   Make a wide grin and then bring the lips well forward into a pout.
2   Blow out through the lips like a baby.
3   Repeat the following.

Will we, will we, will we, wind down the window for Wilfred?

Wendy and Winifred, Wendy and Winifred.
Willy and Wendy and Winifred.

4 Mime the following poem by over-emphasizing the lip movements to gain full mobility of the mouth. This is important. Repeat using the voice. Speak it with expression and animation.

Weather Talk

'Isn't it cold? Look at that rain!'
Stating the obvious time and again.
What should I answer?
'Yes, I can see!'
Really much easier to simply agree.

'Nicer today.' Nicer than what?
Oh, talk of the weather! (I almost forgot.)
'Yes, nicer indeed,'
I quickly assent
And almost as quickly I start to relent.

For what are you thinking?
Are you thinking as I –
'Don't talk of the weather,
Don't dwell on the sky.
Conventional, proper –
So socially right.
Much nicer to speak of the things that delight.'

Be clear, be understood

I once heard a speech on interior design. The seating was arranged theatre style and I sat in the sixth row from the front.

The woman giving the talk was well dressed with a smart hairstyle and beautiful make-up. She was good-looking and graceful. The image she conveyed was one of confidence and elegance. That is, until she opened her mouth. Her speech let her down. It was sloppy. Word endings were blurred and what could have been an animated face was made sullen through lack of articulation. She barely moved her mouth at all! It was a pity, because she had obviously invested a great deal of time and effort in preparing what would otherwise have been a first-class talk.

It is the consonants that provide the outline and cut to the words. No matter how well a person projects their voice, if the word endings are weak, they won't be heard or understood. So remember: *clarity aids projection.*

In particular, watch for:

t,d,m,n,l and **k** endings: e.g. tent, David, kick

t,k,l, in the middle of words: e.g. butter, licking, illness

LAZY TONGUES MAKE LAZY SPEECH

While consonants give clarity and cut to a word, vowels give tonal quality to the voice. Because this book is not an elocution manual, it is not my intention to go into intricate detail on the formation of the vowels and the consonants. Suffice to say that a consonant is formed by air coming from the larynx that is stopped by one or two of the articulative organs of speech – tongue, teeth, hard and soft palates, gums, lips – before it is released. For example, **d** requires that the vocalized breath from the larynx is stopped by the tongue-tip against the teeth ridge (the ridge formed behind the upper teeth), before being released as the sound **d**. **b** requires that the vocalized breath is stopped by the lips, before being released as the sound **b**. Other vocalized consonants are: **m, g, l, j, ge, n, ng, r, th, v, w, y** and **z**. Some consonants use vocalized breath and some unvocalized, such as **k**. This requires unvocalized breath from the larynx being stopped by the back of the tongue arching towards the soft palate and then releasing. **p** is another unvocalized consonant, as are: **ch, f, h, sh, s, t,** and **th**. These need particular care while enunciating. **TH** This can be an unvocalized sound as in: **Thursday, thanks, theatre,** etc. or **th** can be vocalized as in: **this, that, there, those, than,** etc.

Vowels on the other hand have a free, open passage. The lips and tongue shape the different sounds, but there is no truncation.

Make your consonants distinctly, and for the formation of the vowels, open your mouth to let out the sounds. Keep the jaw flexible. There should be a concept of placing vowel sounds forward in the mouth. Shaping the lips will help you achieve this.

The following exercises incorporate the vowels and some of the consonants. Aim for accuracy and expressive delivery. Using generous mouth movements will exercise the muscles and help loosen the jaw. However, avoid strain, as this can be counter-productive. These exercises should be practised regularly prior to a public-speaking engagement.

Exercise 17   Lip and tongue warm-ups
Speak the following clearly and with energy. Aim for accuracy. When familiar with them, repeat with speed until you can speak them quickly without making a mistake.

Use firm tongue and lip movements to exercise the muscles, but avoid strain.

ddd   ttt   (Repeat 3 times)

lll   kkk   (Repeat 3 times)

mmm   nnn   (Repeat 3 times)

bbb   ppp   (Repeat 3 times)

tot   dod   lel   nell

tok   tuk   tak   tek

lot   lad   led   men

bold   helm   land   doubled

better   botter   batter   bitter
heckle   locker   lacquer   liquor
meddled   modelled   middled   troubled
bep   bap   bip   bop
kep   kap   kip   kop
Stack the sacks and check the stock
'Double, double, toil and trouble'
Peter Piper picked a peck of pickled pepper
The old kitchen clock has stopped

Exercise 18   Articulation for short vowels plus consonants

The signs in brackets are according to the International Phonetic Alphabet (IPA).

a (æ)   Angela is angry with Andy for antagonizing her Alsatian.

b   Betty and Bill are Benny's best friends.

c   Cats catch and kill canaries.

d   Dennis and Dave drive dangerously down Dudden Hill.

e (e)   Eddie is extrovert, extravagant and entertaining.

f   Flat fish and flying fish; fillet of fish and fish cakes.

g   Ghastly Gordon greedily gobbles gherkins.

h   Henry has a hundred hats hanging on his hat stand.

i (i)   Ingrid invites in-laws to Ipswich.

j   Jolly Jasper jumps for joy.

k   Kit eats Kit-kat in Kerry's kitchen.

l   Lady Lavinia Luckham listens to Liszt.

m	Mermaids' melodies are mesmerizing.
n	Nattie's neighbours niggle noisily.
o (o)	Opulent Olive enjoys opera and oratorios.
p	Pots, pans, powder and prunes.
qu	Quirky quacks quibble and quip.
r	Running Richard races rogues round Rotten Row.
s	Sally's sister Susie sambas.
t	Trains, tickets and time-tables are terribly trying.
u(ʌ)	Uncle Ulric unfolds his umber umbrella.
u(u)	Puss chased the rooks by the brook in the wood.
v	Vain Vinny varnishes vases with vivid violet.
w	Wandering wenches wear wellingtons in wintry weather.
x	Xavier's X-rays are excellent.
y	Yokels yodel at Yuletide.
z	Zig-zagging, zany zebras.

Exercise 19   Articulation for long vowels

ah (ai) Arnold, Jaguar, far, smarter, car, Carl, Ferrari
Arnold's Jaguar is a far smarter car than Carl's Ferrari.

er (ɜ:) early, bird, worm
The early bird catches the worm.

aw (ɔ:) wardrobes, warm, ward, hoary, storm
Wardrobes must be warm, to ward off hoary frosts and storm.

oo (u:) goosey, soup, rooster, cool, mousse, noodle
Goosey soup, rooster soup, cool mousse and noodle soup.

ee (i:) sleepy, dreamy, easy, stream
Sleepy, dreamy, take it easy; swim with the stream.

ew (ju) new, tulips, Duke, Tewkesbury
The new tulips were given to the Duke when he visited Tewkesbury.

ay (ei) pale, maidens, bathe, daily, shady, glades
Pale maidens bathe daily in shady glades.

i (ai) nice, rice, light, white
Nice rice, light rice, nice, white, light rice.

oy (ɔi) toys, boys
Men with toys will always be boys.

ow (au) Brown, found, cow, lounge
Mrs Brown found a cow in her front lounge.

oh (ðu) Roland, wrote, odious, odes, Rhoda
Roland wrote odious odes to Rhoda.

ear (ið) piercing, cheers, weary, ears
Piercing cheers make weary ears.

air (ɛð) aeroplanes, heiresses, various, fair
Aeroplanes fly heiresses to various fair places.

oor (uð) rural, tours, brochure
Rural Tours are advertising their brochures.

ure (juð) Muriel, liqueur, ewer
Muriel hides bottles of liqueur in the bathroom ewer.

ire (aið) choirs, lyres, friars
Harmonizing choirs; lutes and lyres; monks and friars.

our (auð) flowers, showery, bowers
Seeds burst into flowers in showery bowers.

Exercise 20   Speaking with clarity
LIMBER UP YOUR LANGUAGE SKILLS

'Language is the dress of thought.'

(*Samuel Johnson*, Life of Cowley)

When addressing a Sunday School class, one teacher I knew used to begin by saying, 'Now, who can remember what we talked about last week?' She was astonished when not one member of her group could recall the previous week's lesson. Little wonder. We all need memory joggers, some clue or guide to set us on the right trail.

For the person who is a newcomer to public speaking, the task of channelling thoughts and setting them down on paper in an expressive fashion can be extremely difficult. The brain needs a prompt, some kind of stimulus to get it going in the direction for which it is intended. There needs to be a limbering-up period. Just as with keeping fit, the warming-up before exercise and the warming-down afterwards is considered essential in order to prevent undue stress on the body. And so exercises that encourage language skills can help fluency of speech.

In the course of my work, I sometimes meet clients who are in isolating jobs. There are those who spend their working day sitting in front of a VDU screen, or working with figures. One such person admitted that he spoke so seldom he felt that he had almost forgotten how to string a coherent sentence together. The reality was that he had developed a fear of speaking aloud because he did it so rarely. It was not that he was unable but rather that he lacked the stimulus to speak and therefore the confidence to do so.

George and Weedon Grossmith's *Diary of a Nobody* is an entertaining account of the everyday events of a Victorian family man, Charles Pooter. He relates amusing stories of the parlour games that he, his wife, son and friends would play after work in the evening. These presented the Victorians with many opportunities to interact, and have fun together. What a pity that today television has to some degree robbed us of valuable opportunities for family conversation. We sit passively and watch the screen, but we are away from action – the interplay between one human being and another.

The following exercises will, I hope, encourage oral skills. First of all, they are meant to be fun. Like games, you can play them singly, with a partner, or with members of your family. The exercises encourage imagination, accuracy and concentration. They all require self-involvement.

When practising these exercises, avoid overuse of the same word. For example, lovely. Alternatives might be: pleasing, elegant, graceful, fair, brilliant, radiant, etc. Choose expressive vocabulary that adds colour and enhances your descriptions. A thesaurus provides a wealth of alternative adjectives that you can use. (There is advice in Chapter 3 on choosing words well.)

Exercise 21   Visualization
This exercise or game can be practised alone, with a partner or within a group.

Sit back in a comfortable chair and close your eyes. Take your mind back to a place you have visited. Maybe it was while on holiday at the seaside, or in the mountains; a cathedral, house or park. Take time to recall the place as accurately as you can. When you are ready, recount this memory aloud, either to yourself or to your partner. Having described the place, express your feelings about it. Why did you choose it? What was it that held special appeal for you? If at first you find this exercise difficult, start by describing some functional tasks, such as cooking breakfast, your journey to work, cleaning the car, etc. Focusing on detail can improve concentration skills – vital for public speaking.

If you are doing this exercise with a partner or group, take turns, and while one is recounting their scene, use your listening and concentration to help draw on your imagination to create as full a picture in your mind as possible of the speaker's account.

This exercise can be developed into story-telling. Choose

a scene, such as a walk through the woods, or a visit to an art gallery. As before, sit with eyes closed and imagine yourself as a character within this scene. It can then be developed by each member of the group in turn. Avoid too much plot-mongering and centre your attention on the characters and the situations that evolve from them.

When the story is completed, write it down and read it aloud. Your thoughts and creative ideas have now become manifest. You have used your imaginative skills to formulate a story which has been processed from a memory or an idea. This has been expressed verbally, and then translated into the written word.

A similar development takes place when preparing and delivering a speech. You are given a theme or subject on which to talk. Your imagination then sets to work on ways to present your ideas creatively. Collation of the relevant material comes next, which is then transposed on to paper, and finally delivered as a speech.

Exercise 22 Story-telling from pictures
Nowadays there are so many beautiful greeting cards on the market. Begin by collecting a few of these to use for this exercise. Choose those that appeal to you and are interesting in content, such as reproductions of paintings, preferably with people in them.

Choose a quiet moment, relax in a chair, place one of these cards in front of you and study it. Look at the colour and texture, the shapes and contents of the card. Now describe what you see.

When you have studied the card, become more involved with the subject matter. Imagine stepping into the picture. For example, the card might depict a family sitting or playing on the beach. Envision yourself as a member of that family, a guest, or passer-by. Establish what your relationship is within that group, and observe what might be going on around you. Speak your thoughts.

As you become more confident with this exercise, you can use a tape-recorder to monitor your use of language and vocabulary. Play the tape back and assess yourself for fluency and accuracy.

Speech-makers are very often remembered for the stories they tell. For them, they are a welcome tool, and part of an essential kit. A well-rendered anecdote can bear the stamp of its speaker.

A development of this exercise, which you can play alone or with a partner, uses several cards.

A   Arranges a selection of cards in any order he or she chooses.

B   Weaves a story following the sequence in which the cards are placed.

Exercise 23   Reading and retelling a story
This exercise encourages memory, accuracy and con-centration skills.

Read aloud a short fairy story or the like.

Re-tell it, using your own words.

Exercise 24   Reading on tape
There may be some of you who will prefer to read your text aloud when giving a speech. If this is so, check sight-reading by taping yourself speaking a passage of text. If on playback you think it lacks flow and is verbally inaccurate, then your sight-reading is weak and would benefit from practice.

For business presentations, precision can be essential. Read aloud a little every day and your confidence and skill will increase.

Note the following:

1   Mark where you are going to take your breath pauses. This will help your flow.

2 Aim to glance ahead when you are reading, so that your peripheral vision is aware of the text before you speak it.

3 When checking your recorded passage against your written text, methodically underline words that have been mispronounced or left out, and then repeat the same exercise until you get it right.

4 When preparing your presentation, ensure that you underline words that you find difficult to pronounce. Rehearse these repeatedly until you feel comfortable saying them.

CHAPTER THREE

Preparing your material

MAKING A START

'Tongues in trees, books in running brooks, sermons in stones, and good in everything.'
(Shakespeare, As You Like It, Act II, i)

'I feel,' said Mr Toot', in an impassioned tone, 'as if I could express my feelings, at the present moment, in a most remarkable manner, if – if – I could only get a start.'
(Charles Dickens, Dombey and Son, Chapter 56)

Cracking the ice

If you want to speak in public, start writing. Get the brain working by carrying a notebook around with you and jotting down your thoughts about anything that interests you. Become one of life's observers – and discover the many layers that it has to offer. Study a flower, a poem, a person. Become mentally agile and open your mind to everything around you.

Start collecting and collating necessary information, illustrative quotations and stories well in advance of preparing your speech. This helps prevent feelings of panic.

As you go about your daily work, write down on paper any ideas that spring to mind and file them away. Apart from saving yourself work later on, having some initial material provides a comforting buffer. It can be a very daunting feeling to sit at the typewriter or with pen and a blank sheet of paper, cold, without a thought in your head or a note at your fingertips, when you come to write the first daft. So be gentle with yourself and *prepare well in advance*.

THINKING BEFORE WRITING

Before you start to write, here are some specific points to consider:

1 Know what your subject is to be and how far you are going to take it.

2 Ask yourself, 'What do the audience really want to know?'

3 Will the important facts be highlighted?

4 Will the talk be clear and easy to understand?

5 Is there a strong theme throughout? (Avoid too much padding or deviating from the point.)

6 Will there be a time limit? Check that you will be able to keep to it.

7 Will it be possible to introduce pictorial language? Is it too abstract?

8 Will the speech be presented in such a way that the listeners will find it easy to retain?

9 Is there too much information?

10 Will you use visual aids? Where will they fit in?

Remember to:

11 Use simple and direct language wherever possible.

12 Be grammatical and clear in delivery.

13 Adopt a bright and cheerful style, without being trite or trivial.

Be interesting, be visual
Speak the language your audience will understand.

George is an accountant. He has been asked to give a talk about his job. The audience comprises people who know relatively little about his subject. If he uses highly technical jargon he will fog the listeners and lose their interest. Talking in too many abstracts will bore them. So George decides to pepper his talk with personal experiences and stories to highlight his message and illustrate his technical points, which he keeps simple and uncomplicated.

If, on the other hand, George will be making a speech to a group of other accountants, he may need to adopt a different style. He won't however overload the listeners with too much data. The brain can only absorb so much at any one time.

Talking pictures
A clergyman I knew drew the largest congregations in the diocese. Why? Because he told stories from the pulpit, stories with a message.

Talking in pictures will improve the ambience. Look for places where you can lighten with pictorial colour. If you dislike telling a joke for fear of it falling flat, tell a story instead. It will add charm and zest to your speech.

DEVELOPING YOUR POWERS OF IMAGERY

Read the phrases below and open your mind to the various images they suggest. Picture them as you read aloud the following:

Bright buttoned stars.
Melting moments.
Vibrating motorways.
Steep steps.

Wold-wooded Worcestershire.
Fast and slick.
Momentous moment.
Monotonous monologue.
Energetic exercises.
Marked improvement.
Chocolate truffles.
Thrilling races.
Massive machinery.
Reverent rituals.
Happy holiday.
Mouth-watering dessert.
Slide and kick.
Soft chiffon.
Flat feet.
Jet fighter.
Snappy dresser.
Wellington weather.
Violent storms.
Parking ticket.
Ground to a halt.
Ready, steady, go!
Terribly tired.
The beginning, the end.

FIGURES OF SPEECH THAT CAN BE USED FOR IMPACT

Metaphors and similes

These can stimulate audience imagination, and add speech impact. Use them sparingly and with discretion for maximum impact.

Avoid mixing metaphors, such as in the following. 'Gentlemen, the seed of disharmony has been sown among us. If it is not nipped in the bud, it will burst into a huge blaze that will flood the whole planet.'

Rhetorical questions

The speaker appeals directly to the audience by asking a question that does not demand a reply. This can be used to intensify dramatic impact, and involves the speaker more closely with the audience. For example:

'Why are we here today? We are here to address the problem of litter in our community.'

'What are the main principles of democracy?'

If you are planning to use this form of emphasis, ensure that the inflection of your voice does not rise on the question, but rather ends on a downward note. The former method demands an answer, whereas the latter does not.

Antithesis

By focusing on contrasts, this is used to set one idea against another. For example:

'You played with him; I worked with him.'

'You taught; I was your student.'

'You go; we stay.'

Repetition

By using this, points of issue can be reinforced. For example:

'We will win. We will win, not lose.'

'Pause awhile and think; think what this will mean.'

WORDS/PHRASES TO AVOID

Avoid using affected terms such as:

'on this *auspicious* occasion'

' this most *prestigious* building'

'our most *learned* friend'

'*would like to say a few words* (When you mean '*make a speech*' or '*give a talk on*'.)

'*very pleased*' (*Pleased* is sufficient.)

'*those ones*' (*Those* and *ones* mean the same.)
'*sole monopoly*' (*Sole* and *monopoly* mean the same.)
'*actually*', '*frankly*', '*as a matter of fact*' (Superfluous words.)

CLICHÉS

Try to avoid clichés. Some examples are:
sort of; kinda; you know; I mean; in this day and age; basically speaking; tell me about it; by and large; be that as it may; the fact of the matter is; at the end of the day; let's face it; all things considered; to be honest; frankly; fair enough; same difference; just one of those things.

USING VISUAL AIDS

Your speech will often be more interesting and informative if the audience has something to look at. When planning the content, think about where you could bring in an illustration.

Keep visual aids as simple as possible. Your main contact is with the audience. Don't be tempted to hide behind visual aids – use them as an adjunct to, not a substitute for your speech.

Check the lighting equipment in the room and whether or not the main light works off a dimmer. This can be useful if showing slides.

If there is a programme organizer, it is important to know the set-up and have a chance to test out with the engineer for sound, light, etc.

Slides
Make sure that you keep the message simple on each slide. Code the slides for insertion and index them for correct sequence.

Use of a board

As it is difficult for an audience to digest too much information, very important material can be highlighted by writing on a board or overhead projector and articulating what is written. In certain instances you may need to repeat yourself.

Study sheets can be circulated or sent by post before the talk. Decide at which point(s) you are going to distribute them. Be careful that the listeners are not side-tracked or reading the sheets when you would like them to be listening to you.

The flip chart

This is useful with small audiences where everyone is near enough to see it clearly. It can help the talk to flow.

Three-dimensional objects

I think these are of particular interest to an audience. Think about how you are going to pass them round and collect them. Remember to give them time to take in what they are seeing. Avoid talking too much at this point as it can be distracting.

THE PLAN OF YOUR SPEECH: SOCIAL OCCASIONS

The following guidelines are to help you plan a speech for a social occasion, such as a meeting of a club or society, when your approach to your audience needs to be friendly and informal.

The formats for social and business presentations are generally similar, with a few possible variations:

1 A business presentation may need to contain more compacted information, with the additional back-up of visual aids and hand-outs.

2 There can be a greater need for precision and more sharply focused material, with occasional summaries to ensure clarity.

3 There may be more statements of facts – e.g. statistics and data information.

4 Introductions may be minimal in content, stating briefly but clearly and with vitality the areas that are to be covered and how they will be broached. This may apply more readily to presentations given within a company and among colleagues.

Two-part introductions are useful when addressing new clients, or outside companies.

There is more about business presentations on p.53.

Like most human endeavours, a speech needs a beginning, a middle and an ending. In the introduction, you are establishing contact with the audience and indicating the theme of your talk; in the middle, you are giving the main information; in the conclusion you are drawing the threads together and reiterating the most important points. In other words, as someone once said, 'First I tell 'em what I'm going to tell 'em. Then I tell 'em. Then I tell 'em what I've told 'em.'

Introduction
Think of your introduction in two parts: Part A and Part B.

PART A: 'GETTING TO KNOW YOU' TIME
Imagine that there is an invisible thread connecting you with the listeners. So: start on familiar ground, with something that they know. For example, you can connect through a story, a current event, or a television pro-gramme. It will encourage them to think, 'Oh yes, I remember that', or, 'Oh yes, I've been there', or, 'I know what he means'.

Introductions should be attractive. They don't need to be startlingly dramatic, but they should aim at being imaginative. That way the audience will want more. Talk to the listeners in a conversational and warm manner. Imagine that you are speaking to a close friend who is sitting at the back of the hall. This is an example of a Part A introduction:

'I've had a hectic day at the office.
Everything that could have gone wrong – has!
The car failed to start this morning – flat battery.
The important client I've been expecting all week failed to turn up.
My secretary is having another one of her moods; and the office lease has finally run out.
I arrive home wet through and exhausted, after waiting one hour for the number 72 bus, which appears to be the last bus in the world!
I make for the kitchen and a much anticipated gin and tonic, only to find that the tonic is not only warm but flat.
My family keep mentioning a word called 'Food'. All I want to do is sleep!
But I stoically stir myself and make for the freezer. Thank heavens for fish fingers!
'What, fish fingers again?' their eyes plead.
'Then we'll have steak,' I say cheerily. And I plonk a large misshapen block of frozen meat onto the draining board.
'Thank heavens for the microwave!
'The freezer has not transformed my way of life. Rather it has increased my feelings of inadequacy. The thought of a 'Supermarket in my own home' does not charge me with enthusiasm.
But the microwave oven is my friend and ally!'

PART B: TEE-OFF TIME!
You are now in a position to lead them onto new ground.

From the familiar, you can now gently lead them to the unfamiliar.

'By using the Auto Defrost, you can thaw meat, fish or poultry by their weight.
'Whereas before I bought my microwave oven, it took hours to defrost food, now it takes only minutes.
'The steak is in the frying pan in no time. What a time saver!
'Microwaves have other advantages too . . .'

The body of the speech

The main facts and/or arguments go into this section.

Some people find it easier to write the body of the speech first, followed by the conclusion. They then insert the introduction last of all. For the first draft this may be the easier way. It is a matter of choice.

Know how long the speech will run. If time is short, the talk should be balanced in such a way that the audience is not overloaded with too many details. A longer speech, however, may handle more information.

Make the most forceful point of argument last. This gives weight to the speech. It will also assist delivery when building the talk to a climax.

If a speech is well structured in content (like a well-written poem), it will trace itself through the various nuances, guiding the speaker to perform at his or her best.

Building to a climax

The climax is the site of greatest interest, achieved via the arrangement of points addressed in ascending order, and culminating in an acme of ideas.

When you come to deliver the speech, the thoughts should precede the words. It is the increased intensity of thought, allied with necessary modulations of pitch, pause, power, emphasis and pace, that lead to the climax.

Exercise 25   Building to a climax
Practise the following. Use thought to guide your voice,
emphasis to underline meaning, and increased pace,
power and intensity in accordance with the action.

1   John climbed the chestnut tree.
    Higher and higher he went
    Until he reached the very top.

2   Alec stuck the fire-work into the earth. The paper
    smouldered, the powder ignited, there was a rapid
    build-up of pressure in the rocket case, and the hot
    gases were expelled rearwards. With a sudden burst of
    light, the rocket was launched – WHOOSH!

3   If we are to succeed,
    If we are to win the race against time,
    We must act now,
    And we must act fast!

The conclusion
Audiences need to be reminded. Recapitulation is
especially valuable for business speeches. However, if the
talk is very inspirational or anecdotal, too much
reminding may weaken its effect. In that case you may
like to give a brief conclusion.

Towards the end of the talk, slow down the delivery to
allow the audience time to realize that you are drawing to
a close. Never fade out by weakening the voice. Keep it
strong and sure.

Leave the listeners with something to remember. Not
just by the content of your speech but by your delivery
and attitude. YOU HAVE INFLUENCE!

THE FIRST DRAFT

Now you are ready to start writing your speech.

Enter into the spirit

You need to have genuine interest in the topic on which you are to speak. Make it your own from the beginning. This can help stimulate the brain and get it moving. Your thoughts, your ideas help to create a personal touch which can in turn generate enthusiasm, a looking forward and a wish to do well. If a talk is based purely on an accumulation of knowledge acquired solely from books, your speech may lack lustre and personal magnetism. Begin by jotting down your own ideas and build from there.

Choose a time of day when you can work without interruption. Sit down and start writing, using any collated material that appeals and which you think is relevant. If a fact or an idea reminds you of a story, write it down. At this early stage you can allow your mind the freedom of expression. Whether or not you use all the material written at this time is not so important. The important factor is to get started and to create. The imagination may be inhibited if too many boundaries are introduced too early.

Develop the habit of writing in the way in which you speak because it is you that your audience wants to hear. It may also help your ideas to flow more easily.

THE SECOND DRAFT

This is the stage at which you groom your speech. Before you begin, reread your first draft and then ask yourself the following questions:

1 How do I view myself?

2 Who are my audience?

3 How do I view them?

4 How would I like them to view me?

5 What will my audience gain from my speech?

6 What do I hope to gain from my speech?

These points are ways of helping you to link with your audience before you've even seen them. Keep these thoughts at the back of your mind as you prepare your second draft.

Now you are in the strong position of directing your speech in the way in which you would like it to go. The groundwork has been prepared in draft one and you are ready to move on.

You may at this stage of development need to rewrite most of your existing material. However, with the main ideas of your speech set down on paper in the first draft, this should not prove to be such a daunting task, and with writing practice these skills can improve. Now is the time to determine an outline. You might ask yourself, 'What is my theme? How far do I want to take it?' Keep within the parameters that you set yourself. In the original draft you tapped your creative skills by permitting yourself to think on all sides of your subject. Now you can afford to discipline your work and thus build a format, without being in danger of losing the heart of your speech and the spontaneity of your ideas.

Rather like a play or a novel, a speech needs a beginning, a middle and an end. Because you have written the first draft, most of your material and the substance of your speech is probably all there, and just needs to be moulded into an attractive shape. If you decide to work on the middle of your talk first, remember that ideas or arguments need to be arranged so that one flows into another in an organized, smooth way. They can also be set out in order of importance. A well-structured speech is rather like a chain, whereby one link is fastened to the next. A speech written with this in mind will possess flow and also help put the audience at their ease. They will relax and so be able to concentrate more easily on what is being said.

Keep your message clear and simple without appearing patronizing or condescending in your approach. Be direct, positive and to the point without any abruptness. The syntax can influence the way in which a speech is delivered, so write it in a warm manner, one that can be translated into cheerful speech. Add a little colour by telling a story. This can also help to re-engage flagging interest. It is a good standby prop, an important ingredient to add at a strategic place in a speech that may possess rather dry material. This can be a useful addition for business presentations.

When giving a business speech or a lecture, at least one conclusion will be necessary. Draw all the links of your chain together and sum up the points that you have already made.

The introduction to your speech is dealt with on p. 43. You may find it easier to write this last of all. An introduction may spring more easily to mind once you have completed your written work. Reading through your material will provide mental pictures to help and guide you towards writing an opening.

Avoid overloading a speech with too much information as this can be difficult for an audience to retain. If there is a necessity to provide copious facts, figures, statistics, etc. you can give handouts where and when appropriate, or as an addition to visual aids. Make a note of where you are going to use your visual aids and/or handout sheets and demonstration objects.

When the second draft is completed, put it away in a drawer and forget it for a few days. Come back to it at a later date and you will review it afresh. This is the time to edit your speech and delete unnecessary material. Remember that a short, well-structured speech is preferable to one that is longer but less memorable.

Tape-record your speech, listen to yourself objectively and criticize your format from that. This also provides a good opportunity to time it and any alterations in length or pace of delivery can now be made.

The following is a summary of points to bear in mind.

The second draft: specific points to think about
Look back to p.37, the specific points you were invited to think about before you started to plan your speech. How far have you been able to follow those guidelines?

1 Do you know what your subject is and how far you are going to take it?

2 Ask yourself, 'Am I telling the audience what they really want to know?'

3 Are the important facts highlighted?

4 Is there a strong theme throughout? Have you avoided too much padding or deviating from the point?

5 Will you be able to keep within a time limit?

6 Has it been possible to introduce pictorial language or is the speech too abstract?

7 Is the speech presented in a way that the listeners will find easy to understand and retain?

THE FINAL DRAFT

To read or not to read?
By the time you reach this third and final stage of written preparation, you will be quite familiar with the text of your speech. You may feel that on the day of the presentation you will be prepared and ready to read it out aloud. On some occasions, such as business presentations, this may be appropriate or even necessary and there are suggestions for doing this on p.52. However, there is another way. Many speakers transcribe the main topics of the material on to postcards. These are known as prompt cards. They enable you to refer to major points which will serve as cues during your delivery.

It can be very difficult to relinquish sheaves of paper which hold precious, well-researched information in exchange for small rectangles of cardboard holding no more than a few headings. 'Oh goodness,' you may think to yourself, 'I'll never remember anything from these scraps!' The first time you attempt to rehearse a speech, your confidence can take a nose dive as you realize your worst fears: 'It's true, my memory just can't cope. I'll have to read it.'

This can be the danger period: the transition from paper to card followed by the final surrendering to sheaves of rustling A4s. Try to see this as a self-testing time and, if you can, persevere and use the cards. Once you make that breakthrough you will go from strength to strength.

Reading a speech from paper can work if you are a well-practised speaker with the knack of being able to read aloud with an easy relaxed manner. But I think that in some ways this is harder than using cards. You need to recover your place on the sheet time and time again; the turning of the pages needs to be unobtrusive; and the contact with your audience is much more difficult to maintain when there is the written word separating the listeners from you. Some people have to make many presentations, and for them this may be the only practical solution, but generally I would recommend the use of cards.

PREPARING THE CARDS

If you decide to adopt the card method, here are some suggestions for layout:

1 Use one side of a card only.

2 Number each one clearly with a black or coloured pen.

3 List major points that need addressing but resist the temptation to cram more than the essentials on to the postcard, otherwise you may spend much of the

speech with head bent, peering at details that have been written in tiny handwriting.

4 Any vital information that needs careful reference will need to be inserted for accuracy.

5 The cards may be separate or strung together, whichever is more comfortable.

Once you have done this, *practise*. That way you will improve and gain confidence. You will be able to look at the audience while you speak and communication will be at its strongest.

REHEARSING YOUR SPEECH

Familiarity breeds content! Once your notes have been pruned to postcard headings, rehearse your speech as often as you feel the need. (Chapter 4 gives details about modulation skills to help your delivery.) Become familiar with your voice by monitoring it on a tape-recorder. This way you will receive quick, efficient feedback, and any improvements needed can be put into effect.

TIPS FOR PREPARING A SPEECH TO READ

1 Use a black pen on white paper and keep the writing quite large.

2 Rewrite your second draft in phrases and group them by ideas or in pairs.

3 Provide a good space between each phrase. This avoids confusion and marks the end of one idea and the beginning of another.

   Writing out your speech in this way enables you to look at the audience regularly and then return to your place with comparative ease.

4 Write as you would speak and avoid the use of too many abstract concepts. Use pictorial language when the opportunity presents itself.

Avoid the temptation to memorize a speech. Some people will wish to do this as a back-up. However, it is much easier to forget *lines* than to forget the *gist* of what you wish to say. Forgetting a word or sentence can throw some people and thus undermine their confidence still further. Familiarizing is better than memorizing. It allows the speaker's personality to come into sharper focus and the speech will sound more spontaneous than word-by-word rendering.

So, make a friend of your speech and have fun rehearsing! Remember that the key word is *practise*!

BUSINESS PRESENTATIONS

Audience interest is at its height at the beginning of a speech. After that there is a tendency for concentration to flag, with occasional periods of increased interest. If the audience senses the end of a talk, it will revive itself, anxious not to miss any vital information. The renewed interest is not, however, as strong as the initial curiosity.

From this we may deduce that:

A strong introduction is important.
An energetic introduction is important.
Audiences desire strong direction.
So:
Clearly state the title of the presentation; e.g. 'Our topic is "Industry Today".'
Clearly state the headlines under which you will speak: 'I will deal with this topic under five main headings.'

The listeners will have been led and motivated into a more attentive frame of mind by a speaker who is specific and aware of the needs of the audience.

Breaking up the presentation

If the presentation is quite a long one, let your listeners know when you have reached the end of the first part of the talk. This guides them and revives their interest. As a speaker, you should keep bringing the audience back to your attention. Listeners need to receive small mental shocks from time to time, otherwise the whole thing can become woolly and vague in their memories.

Feedback

End by summarizing. Reiteration is important if the audience is to retain what has been said. The more technical the presentation, the greater the need for clarity.

SUMMARY OF PLANNING YOUR MATERIAL

1 Begin research well in advance.

2 Research facts to ensure accuracy.

3 Avoid overloading with excessive amounts of information. Cut unnecessary padding. Aim to be economical.

4 Look for places where you can add light relief.

5 Be listener-orientated. Write to speak.

6 Be simple and direct by speaking in language the audience understands.

7 Write under four or five headings and, if necessary, sub-headings.

8 Have a clear, energetic and purposeful introduction.

9 Use reiteration where necessary, particularly in the summing up.

10 Write several drafts so that you can edit and re-edit.

11 Transfer the main points of your speech to cards, or rewrite the draft in phrases.

12 Mark where visual aids will be introduced.

13 Time the speech.

14 PRACTISE.

SPEAKING OFF THE CUFF

For those well versed in the art of public speaking this may not be difficult; for the novice it can be nerve-racking. My advice is always be prepared for the unexpected. If you attend a number of social functions and think that you might at some stage be asked to 'fill in' (give a vote of thanks or a talk, or introduce a speaker), carry with you a blueprint or skeleton speech (with the key points on cards) that can be used in an emergency. This is particularly appropriate if you think that you are not good at thinking on your feet.

Keep a notebook of amusing jokes and anecdotes and practise rehearsing one or two of these from time to time. This will help keep you on form and prepare you for that unexpected invitation.

CHAPTER FOUR

Preparing and practising your delivery

MODULATION

Modulation is the use of expressive delivery. It can be thought of as having four elements:

pause   pace   power   pitch

PAUSE

The effective use of the pause
Before you start to speak, stop! Here's why:

1   A pause establishes your presence.

2   It gives you status.

3   The audience has time to look you over.

4   It gives them a chance to settle down.

5   It gives you a chance to be heard from word one!

If you begin your speech immediately, without waiting for complete quiet, you lose impact. *Impact is vital!*

Pause between paragraphs and changes of thought. This aids clarity and helps the audience absorb what has been said.

Pause and emphasis
While it is valuable to lay stress on principal words, raising the volume to add weight may not necessarily

prove very effective. Here are some techniques that may be used to give emphasis, along with the pause.

Exercise 26   Pauses and emphases
The strokes indicate where you may pause. Highlighted words are in italics.

1   Pausing before and after the highlighted word:
    The rain in Spain falls / *mainly* **/ on the plain.**

2   You can bring down the volume and speak more slowly on the phrase you wish to emphasize:
    The rain in Spain falls / *mainly on the plain.*
    ('Mainly on the plain' is spoken more quietly than the rest of the sentence.)

3   You can slightly elongate the highlighted word for emphasis. In this instance you may not wish to use pause:
    The rain in Spain falls *m-a-i-n-ly on the plain.*

Pronouns and adverbs are emphasized in cases of comparisons. Avoid over-emphasis when using conjunctions, articles, prepositions and subordinate words. For example:

Incorrect emphasis   In the beginning *was* the Word, and the Word was *with* God. And the Word *was* God.

Suggested emphasis   In the beginning was the *Word*, and the Word was with *God*. And the Word was *God*. (St John, Chapter 1)

Language needs to flow. If you speak it rhythmically, the sounds and messages will fall happily on the ears of listeners.

Be selective when emphasizing words or statements and remember:

'I PAUSE AND I THINK.'
'I PAUSE AND YOU THINK.'

Words lead from thoughts!

Relate sincerely to your audience. Let them see that you care about what you are saying. Allow your own personality to shine through. While you pause to think, the audience has space to process what has been said.

However, while natural use of both pause and emphasis is effective, remember that the over-use of both can be boring and affected.

PACE

It is important to regulate the passage of your speech. Avoid the tendency to speak at one rate throughout, either too fast or too slow. Never rush!

Pace is varied rate. It is the adjustment of words and phrases within the context of a speech. Consequently pace is closely linked with pause.

Remember to:

1   Breathe easily from your centre to help alleviate tension.

2   Use pause between sentences and paragraphs and for effect.

Exercise 27   Monitoring the pace

Practise reading passages from a book or magazine. Listen to yourself on a tape-recorder to help you monitor your pace. Look for places where it can be varied. Ask yourself these questions:

1   What is the mood of the passage?

2   At what points should I slow down or speed up and why? Is it to:

Clarify a point or statement – slow down?

Help build a state of suspense – start slowly and then gain momentum by speeding up?

Pass over the less important features of the speech – speed up?

3   Am I speaking clearly in the faster passages?

Mood is a very important ingredient. Like the weather and temperature, it can change. Use those changes to add excitement, colour and depth to your work.

POWER

Power is the volume, the energy behind the voice. It is the reinforcement of sound.

This is made possible by the use of the resonators and the breathing muscles. If we allow our outgoing breath to pass over the vocal cords in a positive, well-directed and steady stream of air, we can enlarge our sound. The more air pressure produced when breathing out, the louder the sound will be.

When you speak to an audience, the amount of power you need in your voice will depend on the size and acoustics of the room or hall. It is useful therefore to know beforehand about the venue. (See also Chapter 5, p.71.)

Remember that as you do the following exercise you will require good postural alignment, so that there is physical support and space in the throat and chest for breath. To help achieve this, place your hand on the midriff, and imagine sound as well as breath coming from your middle. This will enable your throat to feel free and open. Focus on what you are saying, and open your mouth for the words. This will help energize the sound and power of your voice. Aim for fullness of tone. Avoid shouting or straining from the throat.

Exercise 28   Power and projection 1
Using your largest room, choose an object near to you and make that your focal point. Speak the following sentence quietly and distinctly:

My message is clear.

Now move away from this point a couple of paces and repeat the sentence, slightly increasing your volume.

My message is clear.

When you are some distance from your starting point, change your sentence to:

My message is loud and clear.

Exercise 29   Power and projection 2
Now do the same with the following:

Good morning, everyone.

I call the meeting to order.

Quiet, ladies and gentlemen! The play is about to begin.

Timber!

Exercise 30   Varying the volume
Vary your voice according to the content of the following passage. Clarity of speech is vital, particularly when speaking the quieter portions. Avoid a fading-out of the voice.

The house you visit is a house of history. So pause awhile in our great hall. Absorb the atmosphere and quiet of this place.

Now view the tapestry; admire the craft. A needlework measured out in tiny stitches, which when completed tells of one enormous, bloody war. See, compacted in this weave, how combat sought political resolve.

PITCH

Pitch is the key in which we speak. There are high, middle and low pitches.

When we speak, our various pitches tend to merge into one another and are dependent on the mood and meaning of our speech. For example:

High pitch
This is used in moments of exhilaration, excitement or happiness.

Middle pitch
This is used for general conversation and moderate speech.

Low pitch
This is used for sad or solemn speech.

Exercise and vary your pitch. It will enhance vocal expression and augment platform presence. Practise reading a fairy tale aloud. Imagine you have children as your audience. Make use of pause, emphasis, pace, volume and intensity. Decide the various moods of the passage and foster the different pitches to suit them.

Remember that with each new paragraph, the voice needs to be refreshed; so raise your pitch at the beginning slightly. This revives interest.

INTENSITY

Intensity is the pizzazz, the zing, zip, wallop of your speech! It is the sparkle behind your voice. Intensity is the life force – the energy and enthusiasm you inject into your manner and voice.

Vocally, it includes pause and emphasis, pace, pitch and power, with the added ingredients of sincerity, humour and goodwill.

Spiritually, it includes belief in your message and total involvement.

So:

ATTACK YOUR SPEECH WITH ANIMATION AND DRIVE!

GIVE YOUR AUDIENCE MENTAL SHOCKS

While a speaker may appear to have a few fascinated listeners gazing up at the platform, this is not in itself proof that the listeners are riveted by his or her utterances! An attentive face may be concealing completely different thoughts: perhaps puzzling over the next meeting at the office, or whether or not they had remembered to lock the back door!

By stimulating the audience through modulation, the speaker keeps them alert. They will not have time to be distracted.

PASSAGES FOR SPEAKING PRACTICE

The following passages are for practice. Before you read them aloud, look again at:

MOOD

The mood of a passage helps determine the way in which it is delivered. It is therefore important to establish this at the outset.

BREATH PAUSES

Go through a passage and mark breaks for supplementary breaths, at full stops, and ends of paragraphs.

PACE

Look for places where the pace might be varied. Be guided by content.

PITCH

Remember that higher pitches reflect lighter moods, while lower pitches can reflect more sombre moods. Change your general pitch level with each new paragraph and change of thought.

EMPHASIS

Stress important words, those used to make a comparison, and words that add colour. Avoid being too emphatic, as this can destroy the flow.

POWER AND INTENSITY

The volume of a passage will be dependent on mood. Increasing power by degrees can help build a feeling of suspense and climax. Speaking quietly can also create atmosphere, and is a most effective way of highlighting important material. Remember to speak with energy and involvement.

PAUSE

Establish where you are going to take your breaks: at full stops, some commas, between paragraphs and changes of thought. There may also be places where pause can be used to create effect. Knowing how long to pause develops with experience. Never milk a pause for its own sake but rather use with discretion – mindful of the needs of your audience.

Friends

Harry Trafford rushed on to the platform just as his train drew out of the little country station. He watched its snake-like course, as it gradually disappeared from view. Resignedly, Harry put his suitcase down and sat on it. He shivered. This was not the kind of weather to hang about outside.

For some time Harry sat there, trying to ignore the sharp February chill that furtively seeped through his body. He gave an involuntary shudder – the next train was not due for another two hours. What on earth was he to do in the meantime? Apart from the station master, the place was deserted. It was then he heard footsteps behind him. They stopped just by his suitcase. Harry viewed a very expensive pair of brogues.

'Harry! Harry Trafford! What on earth are you doing in this neck of the woods?'

Harry looked up from his low vantage point and saw the familiar corpulence of his old university mate.

'Ken? I can't believe it! Of all the places to bump into you!' Harry jumped to his feet, and grasped Ken by the hand. His face beamed. Ken laughed. 'I just live round the corner. Dropped by to book my ticket to town for tomorrow morning. Thought I'd avoid the rush! Believe it or not, we're quite busy here early mornings – commuters, you know. Look, there's my local across the road. Shall we go and sink a few pints for old times' sake?'

Harry picked up his case. 'Let's do just that!'

The hat box

Travelling on the underground
From Waterloo to Charing Cross.
Directly opposite to me
A woman sits,
With hat box
Resting on her knee.

Inscrutable, expressionless
She stares ahead, a world apart.
Hand gently rests upon her charge –
Black striped box
Bound with string,
Hexagonal and large.

Perhaps her wedding veil it holds,
Or picture hat in white tissue.
A dimpled grotto of delight,
Shop-smelling, luscious, new.

At Charing Cross we leave the train
To go our separate ways.

She with hat box held aloft,
And I go home to Hayes.

The clock

The Victorian grandfather clock stopped at 4 a.m. on the 21st of November, 1965. It stopped the moment that Richard's father died. He would liked to have sold it then, discharged himself of its painful associations, but could not bring himself to do so. Instead, he compromised by not resetting the hands.

The clock now stood estranged, gathering dust in a darkened corner of the landing. When Richard went to bed, he sometimes forgot to switch on the upstairs lights, and occasionally fancied that the grandfather clock took on the appearance of a person standing in shadow; standing and waiting.

Then, on the first anniversary of his father's death, at 4 a.m. precisely, the clock struck the hour. It resounded almost defiantly throughout the large house. The insistent chimes penetrated Richard's dream. He started awake and rushed out of his bedroom and on to the landing, shaking from the fright that comes with interrupted sleep, but the last note was now dying on the air. The clock nursed its seal of secrecy.

Richard didn't sleep again that night, and next morning he restarted the clock. He reset the hands and wound it with the key his father had used. Listening to the old familiar tick, he felt surprisingly reassured. He polished the wood and some of its former glory was restored, although it was still darkened by sooty shadow. Richard switched on the landing light. It was as though he saw the clock for the first time. He smiled: 'I hadn't noticed before what a handsome face you have.' (His father had been handsome.) 'I think I'll go out this morning and buy a spotlight. You need to be seen, old chap! Now why didn't I think of that before?'

Computer viruses

'The virus has struck again!' Every 6 March in recent years, news reporters have been running stories on the Michelangelo virus scare. You would see headlines that read something like 'insurance company loses hundreds of insurance policy documents, due to yet another virus outbreak'. The Michelangelo virus is probably the best known, and only causes destruction on 6 March each year. That is Michelangelo's birthday.

So what is a computer virus? In short, it is a computer program that can copy itself. A 'computer weed' may be a more accurate phrase, as most viruses are harmless. To date, there are over 7,500 viruses and about 100 new ones are created each month. A computer virus is not a living thing. I once had a phone call from a distressed computer user, who said that she was not feeling well; she had been told that she had caught a computer virus from her infected PC. I reassured her that this was not possible and I went to her computer and destroyed the offending virus. Computer viruses can appear to be living. You can spend many hours 'disinfecting' computers in offices, only to find that the infection slowly returns a few days later.

Where do they come from and how do they work? Viruses are written by so-called 'programmers'. They are written either from scratch or by getting hold of a 'Do-it-yourself virus kit' and just telling the software what nasty things to do to an unsuspecting computer.

The first virus was written in India in 1986 and was harmless. All it did was copy itself on to someone else's computer disk and nothing else.

Once written and tested, viruses can spread in many ways – usually on to floppy disks. The author can pass on a game or word processor program on disk to someone else, who can then load that software on to his or her computer. Viruses hide themselves on the floppy disk and then copy themselves into the computer's memory, where they usually hide. When that person puts in another disk the virus detects this, and copies itself on to that disk, remaining on that person's computer. If that infected disk is put into another computer, then the virus will infect that machine and so on.

Viruses can also go down phone lines with computer data via modems. As a result, many viruses are spread world wide and are highly infectious.

What kind of damage does a virus do? Most are harmless and just display silly messages on your screen from time to time. Some viruses only appear on certain days of the year (like 6 March and every Friday the 13th, or the author's birthday).

Another famous virus, Cascade, has also been seen on the news. What happens with Cascade is that, while typing a document, suddenly all the characters on the screen fall down and collect in a pile of jumbled-up letters at the bottom. This just messes up your screen. Michelangelo is particularly nasty. People have passed this virus around, as described above, for weeks or months without it being detected. It lay dormant like a time-bomb, completely hidden until 6 March. People came to work on that day and one by one turned on their computers. As each infected computer in the company was turned on, all the data was destroyed on those machines for ever. This happened around the world in 1992. Between 5000 and 10,000 computers in the United States alone lost all their data. The damage would have been far greater had the media not reported it, warning people of the danger. Many did not turn on their machines until the following day, thus avoiding disaster.

Other silly and dangerous viruses do things such as play tunes every few minutes, driving the user mad. Another takes the form of a simple computer game. A fruit machine appears on your screen, you are given credits, and you have to insert them into the fruit machine. You literally gamble for your data. If you lose all your money by gambling, then the virus destroys all your data. If you win, then the virus destroys itself. Let us hope that one day all computer viruses will be destroyed.

SPEAKING DIALOGUE

Use this passage to practise dialogue. Vary your pitch level to establish the different characters. The mood needs to be light and the dialogue quick on cues. Keep up the pace and discover where you can use pause to good effect.

Love's treasure

Henry Price, romantic novelist, living on the outskirts of Weston-super-Mare, opened the front door of his house one morning last June, and found himself face to face with the beautiful Angela Culpepper.

'I've come about the job.'

'Job?'

'Yes, your advert – in the paper. I rang – you asked me to come.'

'Oh yes. Yes, of course. Miss er . . .'

'Culpepper. But you can call me Angela if you like.'

'Follow me, Angela, and turn right. Mind the step. Here we are. This is the study where I work. A bit cramped, I'm afraid – never managed to acquire a decent one. Take a seat, won't you? I'll just move these papers – clear the decks so to speak. Oh, get off there, you stupid animal – Shoo! Out you go!' A tortoiseshell cat leapt off a pile of books, causing a lamp shade to sway precariously on its stand.

'Now then, I'd like to take one or two details if I may. I'll just get my notebook if I can find it under all the paperwork.'

'Here's your notebook.' Angela's smile as she handed it

to him so fascinated Henry, that he could only stare. She couldn't be more than twenty-four or so, he thought. Tall, slim, skin the colour of ivory, milky blue eyes, chestnut hair that caught the light when she moved her head. Oh, but she was lovely. Yes, he could see her fitting perfectly into his next novel.

Creating beautiful women was part of Henry's job as a writer. In the past it had afforded him a great deal of pleasure. Now, at sixty-four, his inventive powers were beginning to wane and while his income allowed him and his wife to live out their days in relative comfort, Henry needed fresh stimulus to revive his old writing skills.

'Anything the matter, Mr Price?'

'No, no, it was nothing, nothing at all. Well, as you may know, I'm an author. Have you heard of me?' Henry shot Angela an uncertain glance.

'No, I don't read very much.'

'Ah well, no matter. I write romantic fiction. At present I'm in the process of finishing the final draft of *Love's Treasure*. Now what I need is someone such as yourself to type the manuscript for me. Not too worried about speed, but must be accurate, you understand. You do touch-type?'

'Yes.'

'Good, very good.' (Those eyes! He must concentrate, damn it.)

'Cash in hand as advertised – flexi-hours – two or three mornings a week. Will you accept the job?' Henry held his breath.

'Yes. Thank you very much. I'd like to accept.'

'Next Monday suit you?'

'Yes.'

'Then Monday it is.'

'Freda,' he said to his wife later that morning, 'she's perfect, quite perfect.'

CHAPTER FIVE

Giving your presentation

Your speech has been written, your cards are prepared, your visual aids are assembled. It is now useful to acquire some information about the place in which you are to speak.

COMMUNICATE WITH THE PROGRAMME ORGANIZER

Here are some questions you might ask:

1 How many people will be in the audience?
2 How many speakers are there going to be?
3 How long should my speech last?
4 Will the chairperson or organizer write a brief initial introduction about me, or should I prepare one beforehand?
5 What is the size of the room in which I will speak?
6 Will I be required to speak at a lectern?
7 Will there be a microphone? A projector?
8 Will I be standing on a raised platform or on a level with the audience?

Know the venue and the seating arrangements
If the room is large and the seats arranged in theatre style, you will need to throw your voice to the back of the hall. Acoustics will also affect carrying power. So, if there is an opportunity, practise a few sentences for sound level before the event. If speaking to a very large audience for any length of time, some form of amplification will be required. When the room is arranged horseshoe fashion, the audience will be much smaller: fifteen to twenty people. This can be an ideal setting, because it encourages rapport within the group. Also the speaker can move easily among them.

Request your needs
If you are the sole speaker, politely expressing your wishes will help you to prepare with confidence. For example, if it is to be a small grouped audience and you like the idea of arranging the seats in a horseshoe fashion, send in a diagram suggesting this.

Will you be introduced?
'And you are . . .?'
   If there is a chairperson in charge, ask whether or not you as the speaker will be introduced to the audience. As a good deal of time and effort will have gone into the talk, you will deserve a decent build-up!
   You may like to write your own initial introduction and send it ahead to the chairperson. Give some local background on yourself: your achievements and interests. Keep it short.
   If you are to be introduced, you may wish to thank the person who has introduced you, or acknowledge certain people present (the chairperson or president and the audience) before beginning your speech.

TAKE TIME FOR A DRESS REHEARSAL

If possible arrive early so that you can check on the following:

The lighting

A speaker needs to be well lit on all sides. Make sure there will not be lights shining into your eyes.

The microphone

For rooms and small halls the natural voice can be used. But generally, in large halls, especially those that are acoustically poor, some form of amplification will be necessary. Will the microphone be fixed or hand-held, or will you wear it on you?

SOME POINTERS FOR USE OF THE MICROPHONE

1 Modulate the movement of the head with the amplitude of the voice. Remember that close up, a small movement away from the microphone can mean a large drop in volume. So when speaking normally, keep close up to it.

2 If the microphone has only a small windshield, keep the head about four inches away from it. Speak out to avoid 'popping'.

3 If using a tie-clip microphone, clip it as close to the mouth as possible and speak out.

4 When holding a microphone, avoid 'handling noise'.

GESTURES

Be economical with these. Too many can be a source of distraction. If you will be holding cards or notes, practise beforehand the gestures you wish to make.

Remember:

1   The gesture slightly precedes the word.

2   Try not to lean while making gestures.

3   Keep eyes raised.

4   Arm movements should be large enough to be seen. Make them from the waist with firmness and flow.

The use of gesture

Gestures made in the course of everyday life are natural, spontaneous movements, expressing an attitude of mind. They may arise from emotional feeling, or they may be used to express an idea, illustrate a point, or reinforce an argument.

Unfortunately when we are on show, either acting or giving a speech, our dialogue, however well intended or felt, is not entirely natural. It has been rehearsed. In addition, we can become acutely self-aware and, while consciousness of self is essential, overt self-consciousness can result in tensions which promote graceless, staccato movements and gestures, undermining the speaker and acting as a distraction.

Discipline your gestures by learning to stand or sit still. It is irritating to watch a speaker sway from side to side, or pace up and down on a platform like a trapped animal. Initially and most importantly, learn the art of repose. If while making a speech, you are using cards on which are written key points, hold these at waist level so that you are able to look at your audience, and speak out. This has now given you something to do with your hands. If you need to use an arm movement, your right or left hand is available to do so. Stand with your legs slightly apart, with the weight evenly distributed on both feet. This 'grounds' you, and may act as a reminder to keep still.

The use of too many gestures can be distracting, however well thought out, so use these economically. Let your thoughts guide your movements, and remember that they need to be allied with facial and vocal expression.

AVOIDING IRRITATING HABITS

Repetitive movements or sounds are thrown into high relief when speaking in front of a group of people. Some habits to avoid are:

'Uhhs' and 'Uhmms'
Short coughs or sniffs
Smacking the lips
Biting the lips
Touching the ear or nose
Repeated adjustment of spectacles
Scratching the head
Fiddling with necktie or necklace
Swaying from side to side
Pacing up and down like an animal in captivity
Looking downwards too much instead of at audience

Seeing yourself on a video will help monitor these, or any other habits.

WHAT SHOULD I DO WITH MY HANDS?

I suggest that if you are using prompt cards, hold these with both hands, just below chest level. As described on p.73, when you want to make a gesture, your right or left hand can be used. Holding your cards in this way looks good and prevents unnecessary fidgeting. Avoid placing one hand in your pocket while holding the cards in the other: it looks slovenly and unprofessional.

When cards are not being used, avoid crossing your arms but adopt a position that is comfortable for you. For example, one arm may rest in front of you at waist level, and the other down at your side. Later, during your speech, the two arms can remain at your side. Alternatively, your arms may be placed in front of you, one hand resting on the other. Some people like to stand with their arms held behind their back. All these postures are acceptable, but varying them throughout your speech will create a more relaxed and confident look.

CHECKING YOUR APPEARANCE

Aim at being comfortable and smart. Fashion is changing all the time, so the suggestions I give here are present-day guidelines.

For the woman
Make a feature of yourself! As the main source of focus will be on the face, pay special attention to the make-up. Strong lighting drains natural colour, so apply a little more blusher than usual and emphasize the lips and the eyes.

Keep the hair away from the face, so that it is not masked, but retain a soft style.

Earrings can soften the face and add interest, but avoid the large, dangling variety: they will be a distraction.

A colourful scarf or brooch adds a touch of sophistication and interest to the neckline.

Avoid wearing dull colours unless they are offset by something bright and cheerful, such as a scarf. Red is a strong, dramatic hue, and providing it doesn't drain colour from the face, can create impact. Avoid busy patterns. They are too tiring on the eye.

Check that your hemlines are straight, especially if wearing a full skirt, as these sometimes have a tendency to dip.

For the man
Wear a well-fitting suit and shirt with the cuffs just showing below the jacket. The tie should be neatly tied.

Black shoes are preferable to brown: brown tends to distract the eye. Coloured dark socks should be worn, rather than white. Make sure the socks cover the calves adequately.

For the less formal occasion, smart casual may be worn.

Smile please!

Even, white teeth are a cosmetic asset to the platform speaker, but not everyone is blessed with a perfect set of these.Some speakers are afraid to smile, because of being self-conscious of their imperfect teeth. The hand goes up to the mouth, or the expression remains solemn in order to hide the teeth. If this is the case with you, in addition to making your own routine check-ups, either get your teeth fixed by the dentist, or make up your mind to forget about them, and be yourself. The confident person will smile anyway!

HOW ARE YOU FEELING?

Food for thought

Nervous reactions can inhibit hunger pangs, so that while we may not experience a desire for food, our stomachs may tell us otherwise and protest by rumbling. This can be a source of personal embarrassment. If you think this may happen to you, eat a little food containing complex carbohydrate, such as a fresh banana (not over-ripe) or nuts, prior to your speech appointment. This will also help give you some energy.

Keep fit

It's generally accepted that a good level of personal fitness helps combat the everyday stresses of modern life.

The nervousness we feel, particularly before making a maiden speech, can often be lessened by a fit, relaxed and controlled body. A good physical condition can help promote an inner confidence that encourages a more relaxed state.

General fitness can give a feeling of well-being through better breath control and good posture, and the muscles are generally firmer.

If the thought of working out in a gym does not appeal to you, or your doctor does not advise too strenuous an activity, walking is a healthy form of exercise and, under-taken regularly, can pay dividends.

LAST-MINUTE TIPS

Listen while you wait

If you are one of several speakers waiting their turn, focus on every word that your fellow speakers are saying. It rehearses your powers of concentration and temporarily directs attention away from yourself. This may help alleviate feelings of nervousness.

Speak out

When using prompt cards or sheets of paper for notes, ensure they are held just below chest level. Any lower and the neck bends too far, causing the voice to direct itself to the floor. Speak directly to your listeners.

Quietly does it

Before giving a speech for a social occasion, leave yourself plenty of time on the day to prepare. You may like to rehearse your speech once more, and then save your voice as much as possible. Conserve your energy and you will remain calmer than if you rush about or engage in a good deal of unnecessary chat. Save social talk for the event in hand and avoid wearing yourself out before making your speech.

SUMMARY OF POINTS TO CHECK BEFORE THE SPEECH

1 *Give yourself permission to feel nervous!* The time to get worried is when you are not! Use feelings of nervousness positively, to propel you into action. This will give you the energy and drive needed to deliver a strong, animated speech.

2 *Use relaxation and breathing exercises.* This will help keep feelings of nervousness under control. Correct breathing will also help support the voice.

3 *Be gentle with yourself.* Be generous with self-praise. Criticize yourself constructively, not destructively. Remember that practice makes for improvement.

4 *Observe and listen.* Learn your craft by listening to other good speakers and observing their style and delivery.

5 *Keep the voice well oiled!* Practise vocal exercises to improve quality, range and clarity. Remember to think of sound as coming from your middle.

6 *Look forward!* Prepare well in advance. More delay, more dread! Condition your mind to look forward to the event. Imagine how you would feel if, after all your hard homework, the speech was cancelled at the last minute.

7 *'With all good wishes for a happy speech.'* Greet your audience with pleasure. Let them see through your animated language and expression that you are glad to be there.

8 *Give yourself a 'facial'.* Practise facial exercises to tone the muscles and help you relax. Rehearse speaking in warm tones. Imagine giving a talk on the radio. Use a 'vocal smile' to express yourself.

9 *Physical awareness.* Easy, relaxed bearing will help

promote a feeling of well-being. It will transmit to the audience an air of confidence. Release tension in the shoulders and neck by practising Exercises 2, 3 and 4 in Chapter 2.

10 *Irritating habits.* Watching yourself on a video will give you feedback. Alternatively, you could ask a close friend to tell you what they are. A test of real friendship!

11 *Appearance.* Wear clothes that are comfortable, but smart. Choose colours and styles that are flattering and provide some interest; for example, an arresting tie for the man, an unusual scarf for the woman. A woman should take special care with her make-up. Lighting can drain colour. Make sure that the face is powdered, to avoid shine.

12 *Arrive in good time.* If you have been able to liaise with the programme organizer you will know whether or not you can run through a few last-minute preparations such as checking for lighting and sound.

13 *Be prepared.* Inevitably, there will be a 'Question Time' at the end of the evening.

WHEN YOU WALK ONTO THE PLATFORM . . .

Make a good first impression
If walking to a platform, adopt an easy gait. Arms swinging naturally; body straight.

Give your audience your best wishes from word one. Show them that you are happy to be there, by wearing a relaxed warm expression. It is easy and understandable to appear stern-faced when nervous. The facial muscles can get tight. Practising a few mouth, lip and tongue exercises beforehand can help. (See Chapter 2, pp.24 and 27.)

Animate your body movements

The audience needs a sense of direction, a feeling that the speaker is in charge and can be trusted. Positive body language can help achieve this.

If using a lectern, place your notes on it with a quick glance down, and then look at your audience. Remember to keep the eyes up as much as possible and certainly during the introduction, when you should be looking up at the audience.

Smile as you speak

Smile as you make your opening remarks. This is a very difficult thing to do, but necessary. Thereafter use a dimpling of the face. Imagine having a face lift! The cheeks and lips are slightly raised, as though you are about to smile. This way you appear more approachable and attractive.

Focusing on your audience

When there is a large audience present, it is sometimes difficult to know where to look when making a speech. If there is strong stage lighting, it is unlikely that you will be able to see your audience, in which case, individual eye contact is impossible. If there is a central exit light at the back of the hall, use that as your main focus point. In between times the eyes can travel to the right-hand side of the hall and then the left, always homing back to the exit sign. This gives the illusion of looking at your audience.

Best man?

If you are acting as best man at a wedding, make sure the jokes of your speech are acceptable to guests of all ages. Don't risk embarrassing anyone on what should be a delightful occasion.

ANY QUESTIONS?

This is your chance to get positive feedback from the audience. If there is an efficient chairperson present, he or she will monitor the action. Alternatively, engage one or two friends or colleagues to set the ball rolling.

Have an idea in your mind of the type of questions you may be asked, including the tough ones. If you don't know an answer, say so and open it to the floor.

Prepare your answer as the question is being asked. Try to be one step ahead. Be as precise as possible.

If a question is asked too quietly, repeat it for the sake of the audience. Equally important, rephrase a question that has been poorly expressed.

Get an idea beforehand as to the length of the question time. When it is nearly over prepare your audience: 'I think we have time for two more questions.'

If there is an awkward customer in the audience, try to remain calm. If he or she is a persistent heckler, you can suggest that they stay behind afterwards to discuss the subject further. That gets rid of them temporarily and minimizes the disruption.

Encouraging listeners to write in their questions may prove a little dull and lacking in spontaneity.

If it is appropriate, you can throw in the odd question yourself. This can keep things going and add stimulus.

ACCEPTING COMPLIMENTS

Some people find it hard to accept compliments. They feel uncomfortable, become self-effacing, and embarrassed. Unused to praise, they dismiss, deny or overlook the giver's good opinion. These are negative and rejecting responses to compliments that have been given in good faith. Pleased to receive them, confident speakers will courteously respond to plaudits by accepting them with grace and charm.

If you are commended, return the compliment by accepting it. Retain eye contact with the giver, and express your gratitude with warmth and sincerity. A simple 'Thank you' or 'Thank you, I appreciate that' can be sufficient.

TAKING THE CHAIR

With so many beautiful furniture shops around, it is difficult to imagine a time when chairs were rare. In the Middle Ages, however, it was more common for people to sit on benches or stools, because there was a dearth of chairs. The word 'chairman' probably originates from those days when, because of this scarcity, a chair was specifically laid aside at meetings for the one who was to preside over events.

An effective chairperson (as a chairman is now called) is rather like a good parent. He or she casts a caring eye over their charge without interfering on all fronts. They allow events to develop democratically, without denying the right of self-expression and freedom. They are firm without being authoritarian and crushing in their role, and they see that there is fair play.

If you consider becoming a chairperson, ask yourself these questions:

1 Have I got leadership skills?
2 How do I function in a group setting?
3 Am I patient?
4 Am I assertive?
5 Do I possess a sense of fair play?
6 Am I methodical?

You will have some idea what your communication skills are like from past records at school and college, or at work.

Of course, we don't always see ourselves as others view us, but we often have a pretty good idea. If you are unsure as to whether or not you are fitted for the job, pluck up courage and ask one or two good friends how you come across and encourage them to suggest areas where they think you could improve. For example, you may be assertive in some areas, but impatient or short-tempered in others. There are times when we may justify certain traits within ourselves, without stopping to re-evaluate our viewpoint.

While you may not have taken a front-line position in the past, consider accepting an offer to take the chair.

One woman I knew was very shy. It was a great surprise to her, therefore, when she was asked to preside over a social gathering. After much hesitation and trepidation, she accepted and was a success. Her more positive characteristics (such as her conscientiousness) came to the fore, giving her the strength to carry out the job well. While retaining her unassuming manner, she was quietly effective. The person who had asked her to take over at short notice had recognized these qualities.

The principal duties of the chairperson are to keep order, to deal with relevant business, to say who shall speak, and to put resolutions to the vote. The chairperson declares the opening and closing of meetings and is the general overseer of the proceedings. If there are speakers, they should always address the chairperson first before commencing their speech, often as Mr Chairman or Madam Chairwoman.

The chairperson will follow an agenda. One such agenda may include: a welcome and reasons for the meeting; apologies for absence; the minutes of the last meeting (which will have been taken down by the secretary); matters arising from the last meeting; reports (such a a treasurer's or representative's report); points that may arise from these reports; any other business; the date set for the next meeting.

Introducing a speaker

If you are introducing a speaker, do it with momentum.

Here are some suggestions:

1   Say his or her name strongly, clearly and slowly. This gives the audience time to digest the information.

2   Introduce the person with enthusiasm and warmth.

3   Include him or her in your body language. Look at the person briefly and turn yourself in their direction at least once. Practise swivelling your body round, using the feet as a pivot.

4   'Ladies and gentlemen, John Smith.' As you speak, include an arm gesture at this point. Small movements look awkward and will not be seen at the back. Use a wide gesture and let it flow from the waist. Practise until this comes naturally.

5   Make sure that your voice does not drop when your body is turned away from the audience.

EXAMPLE 1

Stand and wait for quiet. Speak clearly with adequate volume.

'Good afternoon, ladies. I have much pleasure in introducing Sylvia Grove, who is going to show us how to make an attractive dining-table centre-piece.

'Sylvia has worked as a florist for many years. Her flair and ability to create floral designs have made her an authority on this subject. I think many of you will be familiar with the television series *Floral Art*, which she presents every month.

'With Christmas on the way and plenty to do, what better time to gather some useful hints on how to make our homes bright and colourful for the festive season.

'Please will you give a warm welcome to Sylvia Grove.'

EXAMPLE 2

'Good afternoon. I'd like to welcome to our university Professor David Kennedy, who is going to talk about methods of eradication of the malarial vector *Anopheles gambiae*.

'Professor Kennedy gained his PhD in Malarial Parasitology at Birmingham University and has spent six years in The Gambia working on low-technology mosquito control programmes.

'David . . . over to you.'

Thanking the speaker

If you make the introduction, it is important that you listen carefully to everything the speaker has to say. You can then include in your vote of thanks several points of interest that may have been made during the speech.

Avoid a eulogistic vote of thanks. This can be embarrassing for the speaker, and may not be in accordance with the views of the audience.

If the speech was poor, a polite but short vote of thanks will suffice. This avoids embarrassment all round, as the speaker may know his or her performance was weak, and any hypocrisy will most likely be detected.

Your vote of thanks can be formal:

'I would like to propose a vote of thanks to Mr Jones for speaking to us this evening,' etc. or:

'On behalf of our committee, I would like to thank Mr Jones,' etc. or you can be informal:

'I would like to thank Philip Jones,' etc.

SUMMARY OF CHAIRPERSON'S DUTIES

As a chairperson, you will lead events, so remember:

1   Learn all the rules and procedures before starting out. Revise them thoroughly. Ensure that you are

told about relevant issues that need addressing. The secretary deals with the minutes, but you should look at these prior to a meeting.

2   Arrive in good time to make any preparations.

3   Be firm but friendly.

4   Keep to the agenda and be succinct. Avoid straying from the point. Use interim summaries to help you and to guide members.

5   Deal kindly and encouragingly with those people who are shy at speaking out in a group. Sometimes it is they who can contribute most.

6   Aim to foster a wide spread of opinions. Some people love to talk for talking's sake, and meetings can provide the perfect opportunity for this to happen. Be polite but firm. Suggest to them that someone else might like to express their view. If no one is forthcoming, continue to the next piece of business.

7   Be aware of the needs of those present. Meetings can be very protracted and boring, so keep up the pace but avoid rushing. Be firm, and guided by what is going on around you. Maintain good eye contact with those present.

8   As a chairperson, you may be expected to host visiting speakers. Ensure that they are made to feel comfortable. You may have liaised with them before their arrival (see 'Communicate with the Programme Organizer' on p.70). Ensure that the seating and microphones are arranged correctly and are suitable for the speaker's needs. If it is practically possible, let them acclimatize themselves to the setting in which they will speak.

9   Ensure that you know the speaker's names and that the pronunciation is correct, so that when you introduce them to the audience, you get it right.

10 You may know the length of the speech or speeches in advance, but it is an idea to double-check with those concerned, particularly if there are several talks taking place. This can preempt any future embarrassment should a speaker over-run his or her time.

11 If a speech does over-run or is exceptionally tedious, you can scribble a note signalling the speaker to wind up as soon as possible. You are justified in doing so, if you have indicated the time limit in advance.

12 At question time following a speech, questions may either go through you as chair, or be directly addressed to the speaker. If there is aggravation caused by an audience member you can intervene, but avoid unnecessary nannying.

13 Remember to send a letter of thanks to a visiting speaker, and possibly travelling expenses if required.

GIVING READINGS

Reading from the Bible

If you are asked to read the lesson aloud at a church service, treat the Bible as you would any other book. Make sense of what you read. Use imagination to colour and enhance mood, for it is rich in drama, poetry and pathos.

Although there are many serious and deep passages in the Bible, it should not be handled with kid gloves, or its words spoken with a 'special' voice. I have heard some clergy and readers overlay the words of a biblical passage with soporific, chant-like tones. Delivered in this manner, the message becomes blurred and the congregation bored. Conversely, I have heard the Bible read with meaning, energy and sensitivity.

Modern versions of the Bible are now frequently used. However, the Authorized Version, with its beautiful use of language, is still read in some of the more traditional church services.

Use your modulatory skills to bring the following passages to life. The psalm is reflective and comforting in mood. The St Luke passage tells a poignant story of parental love. In both pieces keep in touch with the sense of what is being said; establish the varying moods, and this will help you to feel more involved with what is written.

Psalm 23

The Lord is my shepherd; I shall not want.

He maketh me to lie down in green pastures:
He leadeth me beside the still waters.

He restoreth my soul:
He leadeth me in the paths of righteousness for his name's
   sake.

Yea, though I walk through the valley of the shadow of
   death,
I will fear no evil; for thou art with me;
Thy rod and thy staff, they comfort me.

Thou preparest a table before me in the presence of mine
   enemies:
Thou anointest my head with oil; my cup runneth over.

Surely goodness and mercy shall follow me all the days of
   my life:
And I will dwell in the house of the Lord for ever.

St Luke: Chapter 15

A certain man had two sons:

And the younger of them said to his father, 'Father, give
   me the portion of goods that falleth to me.' And he
   divided unto them his living.

And not many days after the younger son gathered all together, and took his journey into a far country, and there wasted his substance with riotous living.

And when he had spent all, there arose a mighty famine in that land; and he began to be in want.

And he went and joined himself to a citizen of that country; and he sent him into his fields to feed swine.

And he would fain have filled his belly with the husks that the swine did eat: and no man gave unto him.

And when he came to himself, he said, 'How many hired servants of my father's have bread enough and to spare, and I perish with hunger!

'I will arise and go to my father, and will say unto him, "Father, I have sinned against heaven, and before thee, and am no more worthy to be called thy son: make me as one of thy hired servants."

And he arose, and came to his father. But when he was yet a great way off, his father saw him, and had compassion, and ran, and fell on his neck, and kissed him.

And the son said unto him, 'Father, I have sinned against heaven, and in thy sight, and am no more worthy to be called thy son.'

But the father said to his servants, 'Bring forth the best robe, and put it on him; and put a ring on his hand, and shoes on his feet: and bring hither the fatted calf, and kill it; and let us eat, and be merry: for this my son was dead, and is alive again; he was lost, and is found.' And they began to be merry.

Now his elder son was in the field: and as he came and drew nigh to the house, he heard musick and dancing.

And he called one of the servants, and asked what these things meant.

And he said unto him, 'Thy brother is come; and thy father hath killed the fatted calf, because he hath received him safe and sound.'

And he was angry, and would not go in: therefore came his father out, and intreated him.

And he answering said to his father, 'Lo, these many years do I serve thee, neither transgressed I at any time thy commandment: and yet thou never gavest me a kid, that I might make merry with my friends: but as soon as thy son was come, which hath devoured thy living with harlots, thou hast killed for him the fatted calf.'

And he said unto him, 'Son, thou art ever with me, and all that I have is thine. It was meet that we should make merry, and be glad: for this thy brother was dead, and is alive again, and was lost, and is found.'

CHAPTER SIX

Feedback and afterthoughts

'HOW DID I DO?' THE PLUSES AND MINUSES

The following are some points to consider when assessing your speech or listening to others. The Plus points are on the left, the Minuses on the right.

Personality

Confident	Uncertain
Authoritative	Unsure
Composed	Edgy
Lively	Dull
Warm	Cold
Good audience contact	Withdrawn
Good audience reaction	Failure to move audience
Good eye contact	Eyes directed away from audience
Fluent speech	Abrupt/disjointed
Appropriate humour	Unimaginative/boring in content
Appropriate gesture	Distracting/unnecessary gestures
Relaxed movement	Over-tense

Voice and speech

Clear enunciation	Unclear enunciation
Efficient breath control	Poor breath control

Adequate voice projection	Weak voice projection, or over-loud
Variety of tone using pause, pace, power, pitch	Monotonous delivery

The introduction

Imaginative	Mundane

For business presentations

Aim and scope of speech given	Lack of direction Vague/poor format

For social occasions

Finding common ground with audience before leading them onto your ground	Weak audience contact

The development of the speech

Logical	Muddled
Economical	Disjointed/rambling
Clear stages of progression	Too protracted
Accuracy of facts	Inaccuracy of facts
Efficient use of language	Pedantic/difficult to understand/long winded

Use of humour	Humourless
Keeping to time limit	Over-long
Appropriate use of emphasis to aid clarity	Lack of definition

For business presentations

Stages recapped and checked; use of interim as well as final summary	Insensitive to audience needs
Keeping to the point	Digressing

PASS ON THE GOOD WORK

While it is a pleasure listening to a well-spoken adult, it can be an even greater pleasure listening to a well-spoken child.

If you have a family, encourage clear, well-enunciated speech and conversation, and help them to extend their vocabulary, perhaps by placing a dictionary near the meal table. Fill bookshelves with well-written literature and non-fiction including reference books such as a dictionary, thesaurus, biographical dictionary and encyclopaedias.

Encourage correct grammar, for while regional accents may be socially acceptable, poor grammar is not. If you are unsure as to your own standard of English, take some private tuition from an English teacher who has a good knowledge of grammar.

In the United Kingdom, general standards of speech and grammar are low. As a parent, you have the opportunity to raise your children's standards of English and, with your newly acquired public-speaking skills, will be enabled to do so.

SPEAKERS IN THE PAST

Oratory first became a powerful force in Greece in the 4th century BC. Public speaking was taught by Sophists (teachers) who coached men in the art of eloquence. Rhetoric was seen as a pathway to personal success. One such great speaker was Demosthenes (383–322 BC). He was orphaned when young and placed in the care of guardians who mismanaged his inheritance. When he grew up, Demosthenes decided to prosecute them. In order to prepare himself for the court hearing, he took lessons from a famous forensic orator and speech writer called Isaeus. Demosthenes obtained a verdict against his guardians at the trial, and although most of his legacy was lost, his success in court motivated him to embark on a career as an advocate.

However, his public-speaking skills were not achieved overnight. Initially, Demosthenes found speaking in front of an audience extremely hard. He possessed a stammer and his voice was weak. Audiences mocked and interrupted him in mid-flow. It is recorded that Demosthenes would rehearse his speeches, declaiming the words against the noisy background of the sea, as a way of training his voice to cope with the noise level found among the assemblies. It was only after much practice and perseverance that Demosthenes finally won through and became a fine public speaker.

The Romans, notably the statesman Cicero, learned a great deal from the Greeks in the art of oratory. They too used it as a foundation for power and eminence.

With the growth of Christianity and the decline of the Roman Empire, a new form of oratory arose: preaching from the pulpit. The Turkish-born St John Chrysostom (357–407 AD) was famous for this. Centuries after his death, one of the prayers that he wrote was included by Cranmer in the 1662 Church of England Prayer Book. Chrysostom means 'Golden Mouthed'.

In modern times a great deal of public speaking takes the form of debates in the law courts and parliaments. The first great English debater was the philanthropist, the Earl of Shaftesbury. Others included Edmund Burke, whose eloquence gained him a high position in the Whig Party; British statesman, William Pitt; elocution teacher and playwright, Richard Brinsley Sheridan; and Whig statesman, Charles Fox. These were among the most notable eighteenth-century speakers.

The nineteenth-century saw the lawyer and statesman, Daniel Webster, give many fine speeches. One of his most famous was made on the bicentenary of the Pilgrim Fathers' landing in Plymouth, Massachusetts.

Abraham Lincoln made his name as a public speaker when in 1834, having been elected to the legislature, he protested against slavery.

Today, with the growth and development of business networks and the media communication channels, public-speaking skills are fast becoming an essential requirement of national and international life.

THE REWARDS OF PUBLIC SPEAKING

Anticipation, alertness and excitement are positive ingredients that should be welcomed by the platform speaker. They can result in a feeling of exhilaration and well being. Use these guidelines to create personal mag-netism, or stage presence. Learn to enjoy what you are doing and your performance will sparkle!

Let your message reach your eyes as well as your mouth, so that listeners can recognize you as an expressive person. Radiate warmth and enthusiasm and this will stay with them long after your speech has finished.

Learn to love your craft and you will be rewarded by an appreciative and interested audience.

Becoming a talented and sought-after speaker need not be a fantasy; it can be reality, made so by you!

Index

antithesis 40
appearance 10, 75–6
articulation 26–30
audiences 6–7, 62

body language 15, 80
breathing 16, 18, 19–22
business presentations 42–3, 50, 53–4

chairperson's duties 82–7
clarity of speech 10, 25-6, 30–1
clichés 41
comma pauses 21–2
compliments 81–2
confidence 9, 14, 17
consonants 10, 26–7, 28–9

dress 10, 75–6

eating 76
emphasis 56–8, 63
entrances 17–18, 79–80

facial muscles 24–5
feedback 54, 81, 91–2
figures of speech 39–40
fitness 76–7
flip charts 42
food 76
full-stop pauses 21–2

gestures 72–4
grammar 93

imagery 38–9
intensity 61
introductions
    to audiences 71, 84
    to speeches 43–5, 49

lip movements 24–5, 27–8

metaphors 39
microphones 72
modulation 56
mouth muscles 24–5

nervousness 7, 13–15, 20, 76

off the cuff speaking 55

pace of delivery 58–9, 62
pausing 21–4, 56–8, 62, 63
phrasing 21–4
pitch 60–1, 62, 68
planning speeches, see writing
    speeches
posture 22
power and projection 21–2, 59–60, 63
prompt cards 50, 51–2, 73, 74–5
pronunciation 35

question time 81

reading speeches 50–3, 73, 74–5
readings 87–90
rehearsal 14, 52
reiteration 54
relaxation exercises 15–18
repetition 40
rhetorical questions 40

self-perception 6, 14
sentences 15
similes 39
slides 41
social presentations 42–3
story-telling 32–4, 38
study sheets 42

tape recordings 34–5, 52
tongue movements 27–8

venues 70–1
visual aids 41–2
vocabulary 32, 33
vowels 10, 27, 28–30

weddings 80
words to avoid 40–1
writing speeches 42–51
    body of the speech 45
    climax 45–6
    collating information 36–7
    conclusion 46
    final draft 50–1
    first draft 46–7
    introductions 43–5, 49
    second draft 47–50